A wonderful book on Christian le
beneficial to those just starting ot
experience. Buy it, read it and put
pages into practice.
Gavin Calver, Director of Mission, Evangelical Alliance

Cultures and situations change: the principles that underpin
godly leadership do not. This exploration of Joshua's leadership
provides a rich resource for those intent on pursuing twenty-first-
century leadership with integrity.
Jill Garrett, Executive Director, Tentpeg Consulting

This book is chock-full of practical wisdom and powerful
applications for leaders. The author helps us walk with Joshua
as he establishes purpose, casts vision, dispenses hope, makes
mistakes and learns lessons, and – most of all – sees God at work.
Derek Tidball loves Joshua, understands church leadership inside
out and believes the same can be true for you and your leadership
today.
Marcus Honeysett, Director of Living Leadership

Looking for a book to give to someone starting out as a leader?
Then this is a great one to encourage them on that journey.
Biblical, practical and wise, it offers insights that will help in
the wonderful privilege and complex demands of leadership.
James Lawrence, Leadership Principal, CPAS

In this fast-changing world, the church needs leaders with their
heads screwed on and hearts on fire, who draw inspiration from
deep wells of prayer and from reflecting on Scripture. In this
brilliant book, Derek Tidball has given us a feast, drawing on
the life and leadership of Joshua to help us lead better today.
I commend this fantastic book to you with enthusiasm.
*Mark Russell, CEO of Church Army and Member of the Archbishops'
Council of the Church of England*

lead
like
joshua

lessons
for today

derek
tidball

INTER-VARSITY PRESS
36 Causton Street, London SW1P 4ST, England
Email: ivp@ivpbooks.com
Website: www.ivpbooks.com

First published 2017

British Library Cataloguing-in-Publication Data
A catalogue record for this book is available from the British Library.

ISBN: 978-1-78359-554-9
eBook ISBN: 978-1-78359-555-6

Set in Dante 12/15pt
Typeset in Great Britain by CRB Associates, Potterhanworth, Lincolnshire
Printed in Great Britain by Ashford Colour Press Ltd, Gosport, Hampshire

*Inter-Varsity Press publishes Christian books that are true to the Bible and that
communicate the gospel, develop discipleship and strengthen the church for its mission
in the world.*

*IVP originated within the Inter-Varsity Fellowship, now the Universities and Colleges
Christian Fellowship, a student movement connecting Christian Unions in universities
and colleges throughout Great Britain, and a member movement of the International
Fellowship of Evangelical Students. Website: www.uccf.org.uk. That historic association
is maintained, and all senior IVP staff and committee members subscribe to the UCCF
Basis of Faith.*

Contents

Preface

Not another book on leadership! Well, yes. And here's the reason why.

Although there are some honourable exceptions, many existing leadership books don't hit the spot. Some are good at reproducing secular wisdom, but don't engage seriously with biblical material. A friend was doing a leadership course recently with an evangelical, parachurch organization that had no biblical input in it, and when he queried it, he was told that Scripture had little or nothing to contribute to contemporary leadership! Really? A second reason is that many contemporary books on leadership are too locked into management speak or too complex for the average church leader to profit from. Some contain elaborate systems which are fine in an MBA course, but hard to relate to the everyday down-to-earth realities of church life. As voluntary communities, churches have very different cultures from businesses.

The target audience is those starting out in church leadership, either as lay leaders or as young pastors. The book originated as one component of a leadership course that I taught to a group of students who were soon to graduate and begin leading churches for themselves, rather than sheltering under the wings of others on a placement or training exercise. It received very positive responses. It is aimed at teaching basics that will stand all leaders in good stead for the long haul. It is particularly intended to help individuals find their orientation in leadership and to build in some good foundations at the start, although various readers have suggested that even seasoned leaders will benefit from it. It arises from long observing both the success and the mess that many make of local church leadership.

What would I hope for this book? For years I taught preaching and wanted everyone in the class to end up as a brilliant preacher, but a wise American colleague told me not to be so arrogantly ambitious. My task, he said, was to take their calling and skills, and improve them just a little bit! I hope this will serve to improve the skills of young (and even experienced) leaders at least a little bit!

The book focuses on Joshua and traces the lessons that can be learned from his experience as a leader. He is the constant orientation for the book. But it also incorporates leadership wisdom from a range of other people. You'll bump shoulders with politicians, business leaders and even football managers (well, one football manager!) and learn from them. I'm conscious that most of these are past leaders and their successors are now in place. But it's too early to write about their successors. A little distance is required before the wisdom of their leadership, if any, can be assessed.

The writing of any book is a team effort, and in this case the team is fairly large. Thank you to the MTh class at South Asia Institute of Advanced Christian Studies with whom I shared the first draft of this material. There are many potentially great leaders among you, and I look forward to how God will lead and use you in the future. Thank you to several friends who have read subsequent drafts and commented. Thank you to Eleanor Trotter and the team at IVP for their usual careful editorial support and critique. Thank you too to the host of unnamed churches and colleagues in leadership who appear anonymously in this book. I alone, of course, bear the responsibility for what is written.

One reader commented, 'It is an encouraging read for young, aspiring leaders that God can work in their lives and bring out his purposes if they are obedient, courageous and willing to take risks . . . It is also a good book for seasoned leaders. I haven't come across many leadership books written on the character of Joshua (there may be many out there, but I haven't come across them), so this is a refreshing read, very informative, engaging and exhilarating.'

Thank you. May God use this as a small contribution to help aspiring leaders to become seasoned leaders. And may he use it to help seasoned leaders challenge the bad practices they've fallen into over time, and rejoice even more in the good practices they live by, by the grace of God.

To God be the glory.

Derek Tidball
Leicester
January 2017

Introduction
Joshua 'in whom is the spirit of leadership'

If only . . .

Joshua is one of the most outstanding leaders in the Old Testament. Looking back, however, there was one thing he failed to do as a leader that had tragic consequences for the generations that followed: he failed to train the next generation of leaders.

Consequently, after his day, Israel endured a long period of instability, caused by their unfaithfulness to God, during which neighbouring peoples repeatedly conquered and oppressed them. God was gracious to them in raising up a series of judges to lead and deliver them from their enemies. But their leadership was sporadic, short-term in its effectiveness and, truth to tell, often eccentric. If only Joshua had invested in equipping younger leaders to follow him, perhaps the course of history might have been different.

To highlight this one failure, however, is unfair to Joshua. The picture that emerges of his leadership from the book that bears his name is one of a wise, courageous and overwhelmingly effective leader under whom God's people flourished against all odds. The portrait of him in this book draws attention much more to his achievements than his setbacks, and sheds light on his character as well as his actions. He is not a perfect leader – only one human being could ever be described in that way – but he is certainly a leader worth studying and, in no small measure, imitating.

Who was Joshua?

Joshua was the son of Nun[1] of the tribe of Ephraim.[2] But much more significantly, he served as Moses' apprentice over many years from a young age and learned much of what he knew about leadership from him. We do not know why his family receive so little mention, or why Moses chose to mentor him. We do know, however, that the relationship between Moses and Joshua was close, even to the extent of Moses changing his name from Hoshea to Joshua.[3] Both names refer to deliverance or salvation, but his new name puts the stress where it belongs, that God is the one who delivers.

So Joshua spent many years serving Moses and observing his skills in leadership. Moses was recognized as the outstanding 'servant of the LORD', and honoured as such.[4] It was Moses whom Joshua sought to emulate. When Joshua is first introduced, he is presented as a military leader who leads the Israelite army in the defeat of the Amalekites.[5] His subsequent work concerns essentially the military conquest of the lands God has given them, and their settlement. But that was not the whole picture. Joshua had served as Moses' all-round assistant,[6] and in that role had had a ringside seat at some of the most important events that occurred in the wilderness. He accompanied Moses both at Mount Sinai, when the law was given,[7] and on his visits to the tent to meet with God, staying behind on one occasion, having presumably learned the necessity of communicating with God himself.[8] Joshua was with Moses to the very end of his public ministry.[9] Truth to tell, he could be a bit overprotective of Moses at times, as perhaps any young protégé can (and should?) be.[10]

Joshua was, however, more than Moses' shadow. He joined the spies to scout out the land that God had promised to the Israelite tribes, and distinguished himself as, with Caleb, he entered the minority report and encouraged the people to move forwards in faith, believing that God would give them the land, as he had promised, however great the obstacles they would face there.[11]

All this led to his being designated as Moses' successor. Moses publicly appointed Joshua himself 'in the presence of all Israel', commanding him to lead the people courageously into the land and assuring him that God would be with him. Moses made him stand in front of Eleazar, the high priest, and, before the entire assembly of Israel, laid his hands on him and passed his authority over to him.[12] There would never be another Moses,[13] yet Joshua was a worthy successor, and his leadership was both blessed by God and approved by the people.

But there is something even more important to say. His stepping into the leadership role in Israel was not Moses' idea, still less Joshua's, but God's. At the very moment when Moses was informed that he would not be crossing the Jordan into the land himself, God commissioned Joshua.[14] So the baton was passed on to him by God, as Moses and Joshua presented themselves, at the Lord's command, at the tent of meeting.[15]

And there's something else. God not only commissioned him through this public ceremony, but also equipped him.

The Lord told Moses that Joshua was 'a man in whom is the spirit of leadership'.[16] So God was empowering him with the all-round skills needed for leadership, but also, as another text reveals, with the specific characteristic of wisdom.[17] Whatever else 'the spirit of leadership' means, Moses' ordination resulted in Joshua being 'filled with the spirit of wisdom'.

Leaders fail so often because of a lack of wisdom. Right up front, the Bible is telling us that the anointing of God's Spirit is vital for leadership among his people. Personality, natural gifts and all the management courses in the world will never be sufficient to equip Christian leaders. They need the equipping of the Holy Spirit, both in terms of general leadership skills that earn respect, and specifically in terms of wisdom. There is no encyclopedia they can consult to find easy solutions to the situations they face, and, however beneficial, textbooks can only take you so far in leading the living, sometimes unsettled and even turbulent body of Christ. To fulfil the calling of a Christian leader, the anointing of God's Spirit is indispensable.

Is leadership a gift of God?

This may appear a silly question, but it is, in fact, a hotly contested question for some. Our views may not be altogether straightforward, but there is a spectrum on which they can be placed.

At one end are those who regard leadership as absolutely essential, and they would argue for a fairly clear correlation between healthy leadership and the health of the church. Poor or incompetent leadership or the absence of leadership are all blamed for declining churches and dysfunctional fellowships. It is claimed that where there is good leadership, especially that which learns from contemporary 'secular' leadership wisdom, albeit filtered by Scripture, you will observe that the church grows and functions well. In some circles there has been a push to replace traditional ministry models of, say, the scholar-pastor-priest with something akin to the CEO of a business or other task-oriented organization.

At the other end of the spectrum there are those who recoil from such models, and even question the role of leadership altogether. Some would argue that the church is a community composed of equal brothers and sisters in Christ and, while people may have different gifts to contribute, they bridle at anything that hints at hierarchy.

So, before we go further, perhaps we should at least justify why we are considering the topic of leadership at all. On the one hand, surely the Bible demonstrates that the leadership of the patriarchs, of Moses, and then subsequently of Joshua, is ample testimony to the fact that God raises up leaders to accomplish particular goals among his people at particular times. Without Abraham, Israel would never have become God's covenant people. Without Joseph, they would have perished in the famine of his day. Without Moses, they'd still be slaves in Egypt. Without Joshua, they would never have sought to enter the land God had promised. Of course, neither Moses nor Joshua led single-handedly, but in cooperation with other leaders such as the tribal heads and elders of Israel. On the other hand, the period that followed Joshua is testimony enough to the chaos that can result when competent leadership is absent.

In subsequent generations, God gave the people leaders such as King David and his family. No one form of leadership structure, still less a leadership dynasty, is perfect, and all have potential liabilities, as the history of Israel illustrates. God never seems to work exclusively through one channel, and even at the high point of the monarchy, when leadership was at its best, the kings were surrounded by priests, prophets and wise people who exercised their own spiritual leadership.[18]

Do things change after Old Testament times when it comes to the new era of the church? The outward form or structures of leadership certainly changed, with all sorts of new labels coming into play, like apostles, presbyters and deacons. Priesthood is devolved on all under one high priest, rather than being a separate order of people. But in principle, in accordance with the way God works, leadership remained vital and was a divine gift for the benefit of the church and its mission. The New Testament writers are not coy about adopting secular leadership vocabulary and applying it to roles in the church.[19]

The way such roles were to be exercised is significantly affected by their being disciples of Christ, who, amazingly and counter-culturally, came to serve and not to be served.[20] Humility, not authoritarian lordliness, is required. Even so, given the language the Bible uses, leadership in the church evidently has some continuity with good leadership outside it. So we can learn from wider wisdom. Christian leadership, though, remains a gift of the Spirit of God rather than a personal possession or a mere exercise in human skill. When one has the gift of leadership, leaders are told to exercise it 'diligently'.[21] That is grounds enough in itself for enquiring further and learning all one can about how to lead for the glory of God.

Some health warnings

Before we begin to explore the lessons Joshua teaches about leadership, I feel the need to issue three health warnings.

First, the book that bears Joshua's name was *not* written to serve as a textbook on leadership for later generations. It may have some good things to say about the subject, but that is not its primary purpose, which is to testify to the faithfulness of God. God had promised Abraham that Israel would possess the land of Canaan,[22] and now, at long last after a number of deviations and delays, that promise was being fulfilled. God, as always, was true to his word.

The Israelites had their part to play in battling with the existing occupants and subduing them. But it should be abundantly clear that it is God who controls events and grants the victory. The occupation advances when Israel is under his command and recognizes him, not Joshua or any other human leader, as their King. The advance stalls when Israel disobeys God's commands. He is the sovereign Lord, working out his plan and ensuring that his own purposes are served. The Lord is the active agent in the unfolding occupation and settlement of the land. So this is a God-centred, not a humanly focused, book. Be careful not to go away from studying Joshua having learned leadership lessons, but having learned nothing about the sovereign Lord who keeps his word and saves his people.

Second, while we are going to explore major lessons from Joshua, it should be all too obvious that, apart from the 'prophet like' Moses who was yet to come,[23] no human leader is perfect or infallible. That's true of all the other great leaders who came before and after Joshua in the Bible's story. So don't put your trust in human leaders, since they are all flawed and finite.[24] Depend on them, and they may well fail you. Lean on them, and they may snap. Yet learn from them where you can, and learn as much from their mistakes as from their successes.

Third, remember that no part of the Bible is written as a systematic textbook. Every part either reflects a part of the story of God's redemption, or reflects on that story from a particular angle and for a particular purpose. So it is with Joshua's practice of leadership. There are many lessons here that cover much of the ground you need to understand about leading God's people. But you may well finish this book and think, 'He didn't mention this', or 'He failed to engage with that.' What follows examines a wide range of leadership issues, but makes no claim to be totally comprehensive. Perhaps once you've finished (if you get that far, as I hope you will!), you might add your own lessons, covering issues you face which Joshua addressed.

It should also be said that some themes crop up several times in what follows. That is because, while we have tried to minimize repetition, there are certain themes that recur in the book of Joshua, and in expounding leadership through his eyes, I have tried to follow the course of the book faithfully.

So if you're still reading, let's go to it and highlight the lessons in leadership that are embedded within Joshua.

1. Assume responsibility (Joshua 1:1–6)

Let's begin at the beginning. Joshua was a new leader for a new day. After years of being in Moses' shadow, he now steps into the spotlight in his own right. From the sidelines he is now to occupy centre stage. 'Moses my servant is dead. Now then, you and all these people, get ready to cross the River Jordan into the land I am about to give them – to the Israelites' (verse 2). God makes it clear that Joshua is the one to lead the people forwards: 'you will lead these people to inherit the land' (verse 6). So the challenge of leadership begins.

It had been obvious for some time that Joshua was to succeed Moses and, as we saw in the Introduction, he had been publicly commissioned and ordained for the task. Yet now the moment had arrived, did he feel prepared for it? Graeme Auld claims, 'It is perennially true that quiet, unobtrusive, observant apprenticeship to a great leader is a perfect preparation for a good succession.'[1] True, it helps immensely. Any emerging leader should seize the opportunity if it is offered. But I'd rather go with Nancy Reagan, who once said that nothing could prepare you for living in the White House.

Many leaders confess that all their years of training and all their time as apprentices to senior leaders never fully prepared them for the moment when they occupied the hot seat, having to take the decisions themselves, rather than standing by while someone else took them. The difference is that they now have to accept the responsibility. The weight of leadership falls on them and on them alone.

Accepting responsibility seems an obvious characteristic of leadership, but it is amazing how often would-be leaders fall at this first hurdle. What does it mean? We will look at four elements.

Responsibility means accepting the burden

Although commissioned some time earlier, Joshua still had to activate the commission and go to work when the moment came. He could have flunked it at this vital moment, pleading all sorts of excuses: he was still grieving for Moses; he wasn't up to standing in Moses' shoes; he was too old to go through with it; if only he had been needed sooner; and so on. Yet he didn't. He stepped up and accepted the responsibility of leadership.

Some people envy leaders because they think, quite erroneously, that leadership is about status and power, and gives you freedom to do what you like. In reality, leadership is primarily hard work. It's demanding. Some pastors love the title and the position, but seem oblivious to the responsibility that accompanies the honourable rank they occupy. To be a leader is to accept that extra demands will be laid on you, higher standards will be expected and longer hours will be required. The easy life enjoyed by others is not for you. To be a leader takes skill, as we shall increasingly discover as we examine Joshua's leadership, not least because a leader's power is often highly restrained by others, by circumstances and even by the law. To be a leader is to accept the range of obligations that go with it and especially one's duty to the stakeholders in the enterprise.

In his, by now dated but still classic work *Spiritual Leadership*, J. Oswald Sanders wrote, 'The young man of leadership calibre will work while others waste time, study while others sleep, pray while others play.'[2] From a different field and a different age, Sir Alex Ferguson agrees. He speaks of the way 'great footballers and great artists are not made on ninety minutes a week', and points to the example of 'Stanley Matthews, who used to play with a ball for six to eight hours a day'.[3] He mentions how 'the crowd looked at the goal Beckham scored from the halfway line against Wimbledon in 1996 as if it was some sort of miracle. It was nothing of the sort,' he assures us. 'He must have practised that same kick hundreds of times so, when the opportunity struck in south London, he seized it.'[4] His best team players were not those who headed for a shower or a massage as soon as training was over, but those who stayed and continued to practise.[5] His co-author agrees, observing that what separates leaders 'from other helmsmen' is 'obsession'. 'Obsessives can't imagine doing anything else with their lives.'[6]

Responsibility means being accountable

Rudolph Giuliani earned global public acclaim as Mayor of New York for his handling of the tragic 9/11 crisis. Writing later about leadership, he describes how when he became mayor, the city was dysfunctional, with a high crime rate and the appearance that no-one cared for it. Contact with any city official always led to passing the buck. No answers were given to any question, no action taken to overcome any difficulty and no solutions offered to any problem. On becoming mayor, Giuliani describes how his priority was to instil a culture of responsibility in the city's public servants, from the lowliest city employee upwards. He had, he wrote, 'a two-word sign on his desk which genuinely summarizes my whole philosophy: I'M RESPONSIBLE'.[7] 'More than anyone else,' he explained, 'leaders should welcome being held accountable. Nothing builds confidence in a leader more than a willingness to take responsibility for what happens during his watch.'[8]

Joshua demonstrates this quality in abundance, as the unfolding story will demonstrate. Not all contemporary Christian leaders – or secular ones, for that matter – demonstrate the same quality. They're often only too willing to pass the buck. 'The deacons wouldn't let me . . . The congregation just didn't get it . . . My colleagues were incompetent or lazy. The Parochial Church Council held me back . . . The Board refused to buy into my vision. People were too set in their ways to change . . . Circumstances dictated . . .' We've heard every excuse in the book.

The apostle Paul in the New Testament was a model in this regard. He was acutely conscious of his accountability to God for the quality of his work in the churches in a way that is rarely seen today. His eye was always on the day when he would present the results of his labour to God. He didn't want his work to fail the test of fire to which it would be subject on that day.[9] He feared lest he himself would 'be disqualified for the prize', and was prepared to subject himself to disciplined training in order to ensure he wasn't.[10] He was desperate to present his converts 'as a pure virgin to Christ', unsullied by dalliances with others who would divert and steal their affection.[11] He understood the depth of Christ's sacrifice and his ambition 'to present her to himself as a radiant church, without stain or wrinkle or any other blemish, but holy and blameless'.[12] He saw the church as his joy and crown and gave himself to its leadership.[13] Given that his eye was on his future accountability, Paul's leadership was anything but coolly dispassionate, or indifferently professional, or clinically contractual. He gave himself to them and to the task of the gospel, as good Christian leaders always should do.

So leadership means accepting the responsibility in terms of embracing accountability.

Responsibility means adopting today's agenda

By twice mentioning that Moses was dead, the opening words of Joshua make it abundantly clear that he was called to lead the people into the post-Moses era and forwards to their long-promised destination. 'Leadership,' as Ken Blanchard rightly notes, 'is about going somewhere. If you and your people don't know where you are going, your leadership doesn't matter.'[14] For Israel, this was a new day. Joshua was called to undertake a new task. They had a new mandate. No longer was it enough to have escaped Egypt; it was time to enter Canaan. However much he had learned from Moses, and however great his admiration for him, Joshua was not to be his clone. Neither Moses nor his memory would be honoured if Joshua simply repeated what he had done, or led in the way he had led. He was a different person, chosen and equipped, just as Moses had been in his day, to lead in the light of what lay ahead. Rather than repeating the battles Moses had fought, Joshua faced new ones. His enemy was no longer the Egyptians, but the Canaanites and all the other 'ites' who already occupied the land God had marked out for them.

If Joshua had kept the children of Israel wandering around the Desert of Sinai out of false loyalty to Moses' memory, he would have betrayed the commission God had given him and failed the people. His task was to lead them to occupy the Promised Land, by the use of military force rather than relying on miraculous intervention alone, and then to settle the tribes in their allocated territories. Wandering was to be replaced by settling. The rural environment was to give way to the urban. Tents were to be replaced by towns. Leading the people forwards was what would honour Moses, not falsely maintaining or preserving what he had done. But never mind the fear of betraying Moses' memory, if Joshua had not led the people forwards, he would have been betraying God's commission, and that would have been far more serious.

So Joshua's first task was to prepare the people to enter Canaan, via the back door, to the east of the land, and to surmount the barrier of the River Jordan. From then on he was to serve, first as their military leader, and subsequently to exercise astute administrative and governmental skills. By comparison, Moses had never been a military leader, although he had exercised effective governance over the disparate tribes, as Joshua was eventually to do.

As David Firth points out,

> . . . the nature of leadership roles will vary. Moses' leadership is clearly distinct from that of Joshua . . . [who] never takes on all the roles Moses had fulfilled . . . different phases in the life of God's people require different leadership structures. Moses would not be completely replaced because of his unique role, though neither would Joshua. God continues to raise up and empower leaders, but their giftings and roles relate to the particular needs that God's people then face.[15]

The lessons for today's church leaders are obvious. They are called to lead the church in its mission in the contemporary context, making and developing disciples and communicating the gospel in ways that match today and its challenges, not yesterday. Sadly, too many are fighting the battles of yesteryear – whether those of the Reformation, the Victorian era or of more recent years. Too many seek to freeze the church as it was and preserve its practices and culture in aspic, as if it were a museum piece full of treasures from the past that don't quite fit in the present day. Yet leaders, as we have seen, are accountable before God and have to take responsibility for communicating and living the gospel in the contemporary culture.

We should not, however, overemphasize the discontinuity between Moses and Joshua. Some leaders are naively eager to move people on from their present, somewhat settled position, and think the only way to do so is to write off the past, reject completely what's gone before and eradicate previous leaders from the story they want to create. Radicalism sometimes unwisely rejects inherited wisdom, and the continuity of the story, at its peril.[16]

In Joshua's case, the continuity is seen in two particular respects. First, it is seen in the promise of God to give Israel the land: 'as I promised Moses' (verse 3). God was to prove faithful to his plan and true to his word. The promise may have been made years before in a different time, to a different leader and to a different generation. But God had not forgotten it and would not go back on the specific pledge he had given, including the details of the size and shape of the territory they were to possess. That promise was about to become a reality. Joshua's leadership was not, in that sense, doing anything new, but simply bringing to fruition the undertaking God had given to his great predecessor.

Second, the continuity is seen in the presence of God, which remained with Joshua: 'As I was with Moses, so I will be with you; I will never leave you nor forsake you' (verse 5).

That was just as well, since neither Joshua nor his armies could have achieved anything apart from the presence of God among them, as their subsequent experience proved. The assurance of God's presence continues to be the only real source of confidence leaders have.[17] But it is also one that they dare not take for granted. The other side of the same coin is to remember our obligation to stay close to the presence of God for, as Jesus told his disciples, 'If you remain in me and I in you, you will bear much fruit; apart from me you can do nothing.'[18]

That leads naturally to the final area where responsibility has to be accepted.

Responsibility means taking responsibility for yourself

In the light of God's promise and his presence, Joshua is commanded to 'be strong and courageous'. Given the nature of the task before them, this was a wise instruction, since it was constantly going to be tough and demanding. The people depended on him, and 'if he, of all people, was weak and irresolute, then the cause was in deep trouble'.[19] Yet the fourfold repetition of the command to Joshua in the first chapter (verses 6, 7, 9, 18) makes one wonder whether Joshua, like Timothy much later,[20] lacked natural courage and, because of his character, erred on the side of caution or diffidence. That may be reading too much into the command, since we know little of Joshua's personality.

What is clear is that while God's promise and presence were absolutely reliable, Joshua himself had to respond to God's gracious commitment to him and to Israel. The promise and the presence did not function irrespective of Joshua's response. They did not turn Joshua into an automaton, robotically controlled as if he were merely passive and had had a personality bypass. He has to show a corresponding commitment to the commitment God had given.

It may be only a hint, but it hints at something important. Leaders who are called, gifted and fully assured of God's presence with them are still required to take responsibility for themselves. That means employing, exploiting and training their positive gifts to the full, and working on and refining their weaknesses so that they do not hinder the task God has set before them.

Leaders are subject to the same requirements of observing God's 'ordinary' laws and of growing in holiness and maturity in Christ as those who follow them. They cannot excuse themselves because of the other responsibilities laid on them and blame others for their own failures or deficiencies of character. They cannot plead that they're a special category to whom the ordinary ways of God don't apply. They cannot plead busyness, which may sometimes explain our failures but does not excuse them. They cannot say people have to put up with the rough as well as the smooth, rationalizing it by saying that people must know that leaders are likely to be strong characters who may well upset others.

The great evangelist D. L. Moody was known for his occasional short temper and having sometimes to undo things said in haste.[21] He is quoted as saying, 'I have had more trouble with myself than with any other man I have ever met.' I know the feeling. Leaders must not only take responsibility for others but for themselves, not only for the project but their own persons, not just for tasks but their own temperament. That may, indeed, prove a more challenging battle than attacking Jericho or conquering Ai!

But don't let this put you off stepping up into leadership. Leaders are people who want to make a difference. They can't sit still and let things happen around them. They see that change is possible. If you're content to let things go on as they are, you're probably not a leader. It is no use pretending that leadership is anything other than demanding. Paradoxically, however, when called and gifted by God, there is no more comfortable or rewarding place to be than at the helm, leading God's people forwards.

Questions for reflection

1. To what extent am I able to shoulder responsibility?
2. Have I counted the costs as well as the rewards of leadership?
3. To what extent do I take responsibility for my own life and self-discipline? To what extent do I pass on the responsibility to others?

2. Build foundations (Joshua 1:7–9)

Leadership doesn't just happen. It is the product of training, shaped by experience and a result of convictions. Some leaders want impetuously to get on with the task. Why wait? Why train? Why ask the deeper questions? Isn't the task clear and the need urgent? God, however, doesn't always seem to be in quite the hurry we are in. Repeatedly, we see God taking time to shape the people he is going to entrust as leaders, whether it be Joseph as a slave in Egypt, Moses tending Jethro's sheep, Samuel learning from old Eli, David as a fugitive from Saul, the disciples on the road with Jesus, or Paul in the Arabian desert receiving revelation from Jesus himself for three years. God spends time laying the right foundations in people's lives, both by crafting their characters and shaping their beliefs, before letting them loose as leaders.

When you think of it, this makes complete sense. Ecclesiastes puts its finger on it:

If the axe is dull
and its edge unsharpened,

> more strength is needed,
>> but skill will bring success.[1]

How often we hack away with blunt instruments, taking a long time to achieve little and exhausting ourselves in the process, whereas if we had given attention to preparing the tools in the first place, our job would have been more effective. Much of the contemporary church expends enormous energy on all sorts of well-meaning activity, in terms of both evangelistic outreach and social action, but it often seems to be chopping away with blunt instruments without impact. Before Joshua goes into battle, God tells him to sharpen the axe.

Changing the metaphor, Joshua is told to build good and strong foundations before fully assuming the leadership role. Having once lived in a house where the foundations were inadequate, I can speak personally about the need for good foundations. The house was never going to fall down, but it was always slightly moving, depending on how damp the London clay was. It was irritating, like living with an uncommunicative teenager whose presence you can't engage with but can't ignore either. We never knew which door would open freely or whether the doorframe had moved just enough to make the door jam. We never did manage to open some windows at all. And no sooner had a room been decorated than the cracks we had carefully filled in would reappear. Foundations really do make a difference.

Joshua's first foundation

The first thing we are likely to do if we are seeking to develop a business leader is to send him or her to a management training course. In the case of military leaders, we'd send them to an academy for officers: Sandhurst, West Point, or the equivalent for the other services, in order for them to learn the art of successful warfare. However, God gives Joshua a very different starting point. He is to

> be careful to obey all the law my servant Moses gave you;
> do not turn from it to the right or to the left, that you may be
> successful wherever you go. Keep this Book of the Law always
> on your lips; meditate on it day and night, so that you may
> be careful to do everything written in it. Then you will be
> prosperous and successful.

It is true that contemporary leaders in other fields have to learn a great deal of law. Business has to comply with employment law, health and safety legislation, building regulations, tax laws and trade contracts, for example. Military leaders can find themselves on the wrong side of the law if they have not obeyed the rules of engagement or kept to the letter (and hopefully the spirit) of the Geneva Convention. We can readily see why these laws are directly relevant to their task. Yet here is Joshua, about to become a military commander, and it is the Law of God, given to Moses, that he is instructed to study. The occasional bit may seem relevant, but not much. Why this law? Aren't there better things, like strategy, tactics, weaponry and the art of warfare, to learn?

No, a thousand times no! The fact is that Joshua is God's appointed leader, leading God's elect people into God's Promised Land. He has to lead, therefore, in God's way, that is, in a way that conforms to God's law. The only way to do that is for him to immerse himself in that law, as contemporary leaders might immerse themselves in a training manual. The key to his success lies not in his military genius or, subsequently, in his administrative skill, but in obeying God.

Three aspects of Joshua's study of the law are mentioned.

First, the purpose of the law is to lead Joshua to obey it

He's not invited to study it so that he might become a first-class scholar, able to engage in high-flown debates with other scholars about arcane subjects. He isn't to study it so that he can dazzle his followers, or quote obscure texts, in the original language, or even backwards. The law is given to shape life, to determine behaviour and to reconfigure his thinking. The objective is obedience: to keep it and to do it.[2]

The pressures against obedience will be great. Why bother, many would ask, then as now? The subtle pressures to fight like anyone else and to live 'in the real world', just like the very nations they were going to displace, were a constant temptation for the Israelites. Why spend time on God's revealed wisdom when human wisdom suggests the common-sense path to success lies via a different road, forgetting of course that human wisdom has been corrupted since Adam and Eve disobeyed God in Eden? That's why God says to Joshua, 'Be *careful* to obey all the law . . .' Casual obedience will not do. Selective obedience will not suffice. Intermittent obedience is not enough. Diligent obedience, regularly offered, is what is required.

Second, the exclusivity of the law is stressed

Joshua is warned not to turn from it 'to the right or to the left' since this law is sufficient and adequate, supplying everything he will need to grant him success in his God-given battles. The temptation to deviate and seek wisdom elsewhere would be strong. Voices would draw attention to other perspectives, opinions and ideas. But Joshua is to follow the path God has set out, without deviation.

Third, the way of learning and obeying this law is set out
The secret lies in keeping the law 'always on your lips; meditate
on it day and night, so that you may be careful to do everything
in it.' The NIV's translation 'on your lips' is preferable to the
NRSV's 'shall not depart out of your mouth'. The latter suggests
the law is like food to be chewed over, and there is a sense in
which that is true. It is common to suggest that meditation is
like a cow chewing the cud, turning it over and over in the
mouth. Meditation usually involves turning over God's truth
in one's mind again and again. But the sense here is that the
law is 'something that is continually discussed',[3] rather than
privately, silently or inwardly contemplated. The image is of
a much more active process of Joshua and his advisors discussing its meaning and application to the children of Israel
so that it shapes their decisions and policies, rather than being
something internal to Joshua.

In insisting that they continually gave attention to the law,
the instruction to Joshua was consistent with the command
given to the future kings of Israel in Deuteronomy 17:18:
'When he takes the throne of his kingdom, he is to write for
himself on a scroll a copy of this law, taken from that of the
Levitical priests.' The king was required not merely to hear
the law read to him, but to thoroughly acquaint himself with
it by reproducing it himself, in order to obey it. Writing it out
for himself would ensure that the king would pay much more
attention to it and know it more deeply than if he merely
listened to it. Even a king's mind could wander!

A later example
Centuries later Ezra, another godly key figure, who led the
Jewish people back to reoccupy their home in Judah after
the exile, proved that the requirements of godly leaders had
not changed. He was a superb exemplar of the very qualities

expected of Joshua as he 'devoted himself to the study and observance of the Law of the LORD, and to teaching its decrees and laws in Israel'.[4] Meditation and personal obedience are the prerequisites of leading others in God's name.

The Bible remains the indispensable foundation of Christian leadership, and we are required to pay it the same dedicated attention today as was required of Joshua. Passing acquaintance with it or vague knowledge of it are an inadequate foundation, and thus dangerous. As the Navigators' leader LeRoy Eims once wrote, 'We must get into the Word, and the Word must get into us.'[5] It won't get into us unless we get into it though regular, attentive study.

It is to be regretted that some present-day Christian leaders seem to know more about contemporary culture, or management techniques, or marketing practices than they do about the Bible. I recognize that their motives are often genuine. They're concerned to be on top of such fields for the sake of mission, and knowing about these areas is obviously useful.[6] But giving such knowledge a priority over the Bible is deeply flawed. First, it fails to follow God's agenda for leaders, as set out in Joshua. Second, it ignores the spiritual dimensions of the battle in which we are engaged: we're not selling cars or computers, but seeking to bring good news to people whose hearts are corrupt and who are under the influence of the world, the flesh and the devil. Third, it makes *us*, and our ideas and efforts, the centre of our thinking rather than *God* and his actions. It assumes we are the effective agents of change and reduces God to some degree of passivity or impotence. So the church becomes anthropocentric rather than theocentric or Christocentric. Fourth, it ignores the lessons of history, which repeatedly illustrate the way in which when past movements have made successful mission rather than God's glory the be-all and end-all of their activity, they end up being secularized. The motives are good, but the foundations are faulty, and no good building endures on inadequate foundations.[7]

Good leadership requires solid foundations.

Joshua's second foundation

The background

Joshua's second foundation is the presence of God, mentioned in the last chapter, but worth further consideration. It is God's presence that makes the difference, assuring both Joshua and the people that, although he is not Moses and never will be, he is qualified and equipped to lead as Moses once did.

Moses had understood how absolutely indispensable God's presence was to Israel's success. After the people had stupidly made and worshipped a golden calf,[8] God's anger against Israel was such that he told Moses he would keep his word and give them the land of Canaan, as promised, 'but I will not go with you'.[9] God reasoned that rather than his presence being a blessing to them, it would endanger them.[10] Moses, however, knew that making the journey without God with them was futile, and he pleaded with God, 'If your Presence does not go with us, do not send us up from here.'[11] Without God's presence there would have been nothing special about Israel. They would have been just like any other nation, trying by their own efforts to make their way in a hostile world.

Joshua had been at Moses' side during this incident and had learned the lesson well. The key to any success lay in God being with them. He also knew that the promise of success was no blank cheque. It was dependent on Israel obeying the terms of their covenant with God and worshipping him exclusively and wholeheartedly.

The application

The assurance of God's presence runs though the book of Joshua as lead runs through a pencil. Joshua understood that any success they experienced was because the Lord had fought for them and delivered their enemies into their hands, as he remarks on twelve occasions throughout the book.[12] In practice, this usually led him to consult the Lord before setting out on a campaign. Prayer was vital.

One of the besetting temptations of Christian leadership is to think that *we* have achieved success when, in fact, it is all down to God. We need, therefore, to lay the right foundation of trusting in a God who will actively work to establish his kingdom, and the humility to know that any advance in the kingdom is due to him and not us. Success depends on our leading in God's way to achieve God's purposes, and not in human ways to achieve our personal plans. If Jesus, expressing his total dependence on his Father, confessed, 'By myself I can do nothing',[13] why then do we think we can achieve things ourselves? Remember Jesus' warning, which we have already mentioned: 'Apart from me you can do nothing.'[14]

The success-driven motivation of the wider world has infected the church, with the result that we do not always measure success according to godly criteria. If we are to know God-given success, we must stay close to God, which means, at least, that we will obey his word, be suspicious of having confidence in ourselves, act at all times with humility and converse regularly and intimately with him in prayer:

> Trust in the LORD with all your heart
>   and lean not on your own understanding;
> in all your ways submit to him,
>   and he will make your paths straight.

> Do not be wise in your own eyes;
>> fear the LORD . . .[15]

Anything less than this is a shaky foundation.

Alex Ferguson summed it up like this: 'I cannot imagine how anyone, without firm convictions and deep inner beliefs, can be an effective leader.'[16] Too true, providing the convictions are about God, and the inner beliefs are faith in him, not ourselves.

Questions for reflection

1. What are the 'deep convictions' on which my life and leadership are based?
2. What place does the regular study of God's words and his ways have in my life? Am I a 'doer' of, or just a 'listener' to, God's word?
3. Am I daily conscious of God's presence in my life? Are there times when I have been more conscious of it than others? When were those times and what was special about them?

3. Make decisions (Joshua 1:10–17)

From conversation, I've discovered that one of the things that often shocks young leaders is that they are plunged into making decisions as soon as they take up their positions, before they've even had time to think or familiarize themselves with the task. Decision-making is a key component of leadership and one that is risky. As Walter Wright, Senior Fellow of the Max De Pree Center for Leadership at Fuller Seminary, comments,

> [Leaders] are responsible for decisions that affect the lives and work of others as well as ourselves. Leadership decisions have to be made because we do not know what the right decision is. It does not take much leadership to choose the obvious right answer. In fact, some would define leadership as the task of making a decision when the alternatives are equal.[1]

Ideally, decisions will not need to be made under pressure. The urgency of decision-making can be greatly exaggerated, unless, that is, you are in one of the emergency services, in which case it is vital. Decision-making is best done when there is time to consult, gather the facts, consider the options, and when there is no stress or pressure due to personal concerns or a conflict of interests. But leaders do not always find themselves in an ideal situation, and sometimes decisions have to be made when they do not want to make them.

Joshua's first decision

Joshua is not unusual in confronting the need to make a decision as soon as he embarks on his leadership. As he sends his 'officers' – his colleagues in leadership – through the camp to prepare them to move to the banks of the River Jordan, he is confronted with the problem of what to do with the tribes of Reuben, Gad and the half-tribe of Manasseh. They had asked Moses to let them stay on the east side of Jordan because the land there was suitable for their livestock. Moses was suspicious of their motives and alert to the discouraging impact they would have on the other tribes if they were allowed to stay in the Transjordan while others were fighting the numerous battles that lay ahead. However, he had agreed to their request on condition that their men would fight alongside the rest of Israel to conquer the land. Once that had been successfully done, they could go back home to their wives, children and animals.[2] Joshua had been informed of the decision. If they fought along with the rest, they could have Gilead. If they didn't, they would receive whatever land was allocated to them in Canaan, whether they wanted it or not.[3]

But that was then, and this was now. Would Joshua honour the word of Moses, or would he come to a different decision? New leaders sometimes overturn the decisions of their predecessors for a number of reasons. They argue a change of circumstances. They argue that their predecessors got it wrong, perhaps because they weren't on top of the facts. Sometimes they simply want to establish their own authority, put their own stamp on matters. Joshua, however, abides by the promise Moses, his predecessor, had given, as is often wise, and in doing so demonstrates some of the key features of decision-making.

Joshua's decision is clear

No-one is left in any doubt as to what Joshua's decision is. They are to 'remember the command that Moses . . . gave' them (verse 13), to fight alongside the other tribes without cutting any corners by sheltering in the background or sneaking off home before the task is finished. Only then would they be permitted to occupy their own land in Gilead. No-one was left in any doubt as to what was expected. The command was concise, and not smothered by a multitude of words or qualified to death by sub-clauses. Yet, with the same concision, it closed the essential loopholes.

It is poor leadership when we people are not clear what has been decided, or the decisions are vague or ambiguous. Sometimes, in the supposed interests of diplomacy, decisions are deliberately framed to be unclear in the hope of pacifying disparate people and jollying them all along in agreement. Such equivocation usually ends by satisfying no-one at all, and the leadership task becomes more complicated and the issue is prolonged unnecessarily as a result. On other occasions the decision is simply suffocated by verbiage as leaders seek to anticipate a number of objections or questions. It is far better to make a clear decision and then supplement it with a separate commentary, if necessary, than to complicate the decision itself so that people can't see the wood for the trees.

Another interesting aspect of Joshua's decisive instructions to the Reubenites, the Gadites and the half-tribe of Manasseh was that he made its timescale abundantly clear. It was only 'after that' (the conquest of Canaan, verse 15) that the tribes could go back to the Transjordan, and not before. One of the other frequent failings is that we make decisions without any clarity as to when they are to be achieved or who is to achieve them. Sometimes this is a deliberate ploy, revealing a lack of genuine confidence in the decision that has been reached, in the hope that the issue will just go away. However, Joshua's is the better approach, and his attention to detail is exemplary. If a decision is worth taking at all, it's worth taking it with care.

Joshua's decision is wise

When Rehoboam succeeded Solomon as king of all Israel, he foolishly rejected the advice of his elders and sought to lay an unbearably heavy burden on his people, causing many tribes to break away from him and split his kingdom into two.[4] Foolish decisions can have catastrophic effects and take years to repair, if they can be repaired at all. Joshua shows himself to be the exact opposite of Rehoboam. His decision is a wise one.

What makes Joshua's decision wise is first that it was based on the previous agreement Moses had given which, in turn, came from the Lord himself. It was a matter of integrity. Once God had spoken and Moses had promised, Joshua's responsibility was not to second-guess, but to be faithful to the agreement. Wisdom comes from the Lord and should be sought in all decision-making.

Such wisdom, as James tells us, will be 'first of all pure; then peace-loving, considerate, submissive, full of mercy and good fruit, impartial and sincere'.[5] Several of these qualities are evident in the decision Joshua takes. We will look at others in a moment, but note here that wisdom from above is 'peace-loving . . . impartial and sincere'. Joshua's decision was peace-loving in that it preserved the unity of the tribes and the fledgling nation of Israel. To have alienated the two-and-a-half tribes would have been to split the nation before it had occupied the land, and would have engendered anger and mistrust in the majority tribes. His decision preserved unity. It was impartial because Joshua kept the promise of Moses to them without being biased to either the minority or majority of tribes. It was sincere in that Joshua instinctively knew what had to be done on the basis of the principles of leadership he had learned from Moses.

Joshua's decision is respectful

While firm, Joshua's decision shows respect for all the people involved. He respects the families of the minority tribes and permits them to stay in the land that Moses had given them. There was no point in uprooting the wives and children and putting them through the hardship of trudging through the battlefields of Canaan. They were paying a sufficient cost in being separated from their husbands without having un-necessary burdens laid on them. In this, Joshua demonstrates the wisdom of being 'considerate' and 'full of mercy'.

Joshua shows equal respect for the tribes that would settle in Canaan. 'You are to help them until the LORD gives them rest . . . After that you may go back and occupy your own land' (verses 14–15). The majority tribes were not to be dis-advantaged by the minority tribes. Again, this is evidence of Joshua's consideration, mercy and impartiality in the way he made his decision.

Lastly, of course, he demonstrates respect for the Lord's word and for his predecessor Moses in abiding by the decision previously announced.

Oswald Sanders cites this incident as making Joshua 'an outstanding biblical example' of the tact and diplomacy every leader is required to have. He defines these qualities as 'skill in reconciling opposing viewpoints without giving offense and without compromising principle . . . It involves the ability to place oneself in the position of the persons involved and so accurately assess how they would feel and react.'[6]

Here, then, is decision-making at its best, with everyone being honoured and coming out of it well. Such ideal decisions may be rare, but are worth striving for if at all possible. Sometimes circumstances make it inevitable that some people are going to lose out as a result of the decision, as when redundancies are inevitable, when a matter of genuine biblical principle is at stake, or when a decision rules between conflicting parties and so against some in the church and in favour of others. But however hard, decisions should aim to respect all the parties involved, and not just those who shout loudest, or even those present, but those whose work we inherit as well.

Joshua's decision enhances his leadership

We briefly note that the result of this was to bolster Joshua's status as a leader, an issue we will explore further in chapter 8. Good decisions result in increased respect for a leader's gifts, whereas foolish and impetuous decisions undermine it. Right decisions matter because in the end 'people don't follow your position or your technique. They follow you. If you're not the genuine article, can you really expect others to want to follow?'[7]

In conclusion

In management circles, there are two common sayings about decision-making that may sound trite, but contain useful insights into the importance of this aspect of leadership. One saying goes, 'Almost any decision is better than no decision, even if it is the wrong one.' Making a decision means people should be clear about what to do or where they stand, rather than being left confused or directionless. The other saying goes, 'How did I learn to make the right decisions? By making the wrong ones.' When it comes to making decisions, there is no substitute for experience.

Don't let those maxims weigh too heavily on you, since as a Christian leader you do not make decisions unaided, but are guided and supported by the Spirit of God, whose presence has been promised to you. That's why Walter Wright concluded his paragraph on the risk of decision-making, referred to earlier, by saying, 'The *risk* of choosing when the right choice is uncertain is part of what drives me to prayer.'[8] Wise words. Take note.

Here's to happy, wise and godly decision-making.

Questions for reflection

1. Where do I place myself on the spectrum of decision-making between decisiveness and diffidence? What impact does my location on this spectrum have for my ability as a leader? Am I too decisive or too diffident?
2. How much do others respect me as one who is able to make wise decisions? Do they see me as tending towards impetuosity or indecision?
3. In reaching decisions, am I most concerned about myself or others?

4. Gather intelligence (Joshua 2:1–22)

From a leadership perspective, the story of Joshua 2 makes one straightforward and obvious point, but it is extraordinary how many people overlook this: the success of any venture is highly dependent on its preparation. And wise leaders never skimp on their preparation. It is as true in the realm of spiritual leadership as it is in the ordinary realm of work. My father was a builder and decorator. On one occasion when he came to paint our garage door, he spent four days preparing it before he applied the topcoat. Our neighbours wondered if he would ever get around to completing the job. But unlike many previous efforts when the paint had just been slapped on an unprepared surface, this time the paint lasted! It was quality work.

The surveillance mission

Joshua is shown to be a wise leader in that before he led the Israelites to cross the Jordan, he prepared. The particular aspect in focus here is that of intelligence gathering, vital in pursuing any successful war. He sent out spies to reconnoitre the area around Jericho: "'Go look over the land," he said, "especially Jericho"' (verse 1).

Some might have thought this was unnecessary on at least two counts. First, a team of undercover agents had already spied out the land. Indeed, Joshua himself had been one of them. And even if the majority had come back with a faith-sapping report, from which Joshua and Caleb alone dissented, they knew what they were going to face.[1] Perhaps things had changed in the meantime, but any change was not likely to be significant. Surely this second reconnaissance was a redundant exercise? No matter, Joshua cautiously insists on further investigation. Second, some might have objected: had not God's orders been clear and recent, instructing Joshua to go and take the land? So wasn't this mission superfluous, indicating some delay in his obedience, if not a more serious lack of faith in God's Word? Undoubtedly, some might have seen it like that, but not Joshua.

Counter voices might have been raised if Joshua had just gone ahead with moving the people across the Jordan and attacking Jericho without up-to-date intelligence. He would then have been open to the charge of presumption – that he was simply assuming that God would act and give him victory. Leaders can always expect conflicting opinions about the decisions they reach. It goes with the territory. Our decisions are unlikely to commend themselves immediately to all, even if eventually people come to see them as the right ones.

I believe that David Firth rightly points out that Joshua's move was not a lack of faith in God, since, as he says, 'God works mostly through more "natural" means rather than through the miraculous. God may well do something miraculous, but it is presumption on our part to presume God will act that way.'[2] Or as Trent Butler bluntly comments, 'Human spying and divine gift are not self-exclusive realities. God sends human spies' in order to help develop military strategies and 'to convince this people to do what he has called them to do'.[3] So, usually, when we undertake our work for him, it is right to use our intelligence to investigate carefully and prepare thoroughly.

Discernment required

When undertaking something new for God, we should be suspicious of our passions. Passion and visions may well be God-given and prove great stimulants, but they may equally arise from our own well-intended desires and emotions, and be misguided. If our plans are God-given, they will not suffer from being checked out with others and time taken to prepare carefully for their launch. Much church planting has suffered because basic questions have never been addressed. Major projects, in which Christians have invested huge sums of money, have failed because no-one ever asked some plain, honest questions, and passion gathered momentum like an unstoppable steamroller going down hill. People are often reluctant to raise the right questions because it looks as if they are lacking in faith or spiritual zeal, and they don't want to be a bottleneck that prevents the outpouring of the work of the Spirit. Yet 'more haste, less speed' is often needed in the work of God's kingdom.

I can recount a long series of initiatives undertaken in God's name that would never have been started if some obvious exploratory steps had been undertaken first. Someone once came to me with a vision to set up a Bible college in Kenya, wanting me to channel some of the reserves of the college I then led into his cause. But a few questions revealed that he'd never been to Kenya, had no acquaintance with the church there, not the first clue about the Bible colleges already at work there and no understanding of their needs. The truth is that, like many, he wanted to do his own thing and have his name on it, dividing further the scarce resources of the church that were available for such tasks, rather than working either strategically or supportively. If only he had wanted to get behind existing work, rather than start his own, but as a product of his culture, he was an individualist, not a team player.

The Puritan Richard Baxter, writing at a time of dramatic change in the church in which he personally was caught up to his own detriment, advised that when it came to church splits, you should 'be very suspicious of your religious passions, and carefully distinguish between a sound and sinful zeal; lest you father your sin on the Spirit of God and think you please him most when you most offend him'.[4]

Preparation involves gathering information and forming clear answers about the following questions:

- The question of purpose:
  What are we going to do, or what are we setting out to achieve?
- The question of motivation:
  Why are we going to do this?
- The question of need:
  Is this something that needs to be done, or are others already doing it?
- The question of method:
  How are we going to do it?
- The question of personnel:
  Who is going to do it? Are they the right people or not?
- The question of resources:
  What else is necessary to make this happen? Where are those resources and finances going to come from?

- The question of timing:
  When should this be accomplished, and what stages can we identify in a timetable en route?
- The question of communication:
  Who needs to know, and how are we going to tell them?
- The question of relationships:
  Who else is affected by our plans?

Christian leaders have much to learn from those who have distinguished themselves in other fields. Two leaders we have already mentioned have something to offer here. Rudolph Giuliani paid tribute to one of his mentors, saying, 'One of Judge Lombard's rules has served me particularly well . . . don't assume a damn thing.'[5] Ask, ask, ask. And Alex Ferguson (yes, him again!) talks of the way 'most people don't use their eyes or ears effectively', and so miss half of what's going on around them.[6] He agrees that luck is an element in success on the football field much of the time, adding, 'yet preparation has a lot more to do with success than a few fortunate breaks'.[7] His job as manager of Manchester United was to pursue excellence 'by eliminating as many surprises as possible because life is full of the unexpected'.[8]

As it was with Giuliani and Ferguson, so it was with Joshua, and so, if we are wise, it will be with us. Go, look, listen, and gather intelligence before acting.

An important footnote

Of course, Joshua 2 is not primarily a lesson in leadership, but in the grace of God, who in an extraordinary way enables a Gentile woman, possibly of dubious reputation, to be saved from the destruction of Jericho and included as a member of his elect people. Her role in the divine plan is such that she appears in the genealogy of Jesus in Matthew 1:5, and serves as a model of both faith (Hebrews 11:31) and works (James 2:25) in the later New Testament. Let's be careful not to reduce the wonderful gospel message of God's grace into a simple management rule, even though it offers a true insight into leadership.

Questions for reflection

1. What have I done to equip myself to be a leader? Have I, for example, served an apprenticeship or undertaken other training before assuming responsibility?
2. Looking back on my experience, have there been occasions when my decisions would have benefited from more intelligence gathering before acting on them?
3. Do I rely on the Holy Spirit as a shortcut to leadership? Do I equip myself with skill for the task under the Holy Spirit's empowering?

5. Prepare thoroughly (Joshua 3:1–5)

You may think the point has already been well made, but it is worth pressing home. Before engaging in battle, Joshua continues his preparations. Having received the report of the spies, there is yet more to be done before crossing the River Jordan and entering the land.

What strikes me about the preparations as they set out from Shittim was that they were both intensely practical and deeply spiritual. Like a two-sided coin, these two elements are both necessary to form one united, integrated stage of preparedness.

The church of God needs leaders who are both practical and spiritual. It's rare to find someone who can combine both aspects in their own person in a balanced way. More usually, people will bring their different experiences to a leadership team, with some being more practical, and others perhaps at least appearing to be more spiritual. But how wonderful when the approaches are combined in one person. I thank God for a number of treasurers down the years who could read a financial balance sheet astutely and who clearly lived in the 'real' world, and yet proved to be people of faith and prayer as well. They're worth their weight in gold, worth seeking out, and also worth emulating in one's own character.

So how exactly did Joshua prepare?

Joshua was intensely practical in his preparation

The opening verses of chapter 3 contain rich details that we're likely to take for granted if we're not careful.

First, the journey towards Jordan begins 'early in the morning'. They were neither slow nor slack. They rose early to commence the journey, probably making the most of the coolness of the day rather than hanging about until everyone got around to packing up in their own time and agreeing it was convenient to them to make the move. Leaders are usually decisive, proactive people who act with alacrity, rather than passive personalities who eventually get around to doing things when it suits.

Second, Joshua sends 'the officers' throughout the camp. We'll meet these people again, but this is one of many occasions where Joshua shows that leadership is teamwork. He doesn't seek to do everything himself, but has a faithful group around him who share his vision and obediently carry out the assignments given to them. David Firth perceptively comments that however much they were in this together, there is a clear differentiation between their role and Joshua's.[1] They do not carry the weight or range of responsibility he did, and are not required to do all that he does. Working harmoniously together doesn't involve everyone doing the same thing, still less everyone's ideas being as good as everyone else's. Joshua knew the importance of delegation and just how to carry it out. He remained firmly in charge.

Third, the communication was crystal clear. The people were in no doubt about what they were to do and when they were to do it. 'When you see the ark of the covenant of the Lord your God, and the Levitical priests carrying it, you are to move out from your positions and follow it.'[2] This was how they would know which way to go. Apart from this, they wouldn't have had a clue about which direction to take. Now they were left in no doubt. The instructions were not only clear but also sufficient. They were to keep a good distance from the ark, of about a thousand yards, both out of reverence for it and because of its spiritual power. In later history, Uzzah was to discover the cost of ignoring this guidance.[3]

Joshua is a model leader in demonstrating eagerness of action, wisdom in delegation, and clarity and sufficiency in communication. He's certainly practical in his preparation. Don't be super-spiritual and think that practical preparation isn't necessary. It is.

Joshua was deeply spiritual in his preparation

The day before the people were to cross the Jordan, Joshua instructed them to 'consecrate yourselves, for tomorrow the Lord will do amazing things among you' (verse 5). For God to display his amazing power, the people needed to be not only practically prepared, but also spiritually fit. No explanation is given here as to what it means to be 'consecrated', but in essence it is to be set apart for God. Other passages shed light on its meaning and suggest that it involved purification rituals such as washing their clothes, avoiding certain foods and abstaining from sexual relations.[4] Dale Ralph Davis thinks it was likely to have involved confession of sin as well.[5] The total person, outward and inward, was implicated in this:

the preparation of the body was an outward sign of the preparation of the heart.

None of this is so very different from what we would expect of any great artist or sports star. Hours of practice and the learning of technical skills are crucial, but so too is the preparation of the person. No great artist paints by numbers, keeping within the lines but lacking inspiration. The musician who is technically correct but has no heart will never be great. The athlete knows that sleep, diet, kit and clothing are just as important in preparation for the big event as are muscles. They also need to focus and get their head into the competition they will undertake if they are to win. Many a football team has known what it is to be locked down in a hotel, on a carefully regulated diet, separated from wives and family, and to have their strip washed and boots cleaned before the big match. Details matter. All great artists and sports stars pay attention to the inward spirit as much as to the external practicalities. If that's the price they pay for excellence, should we expect to pay any lesser price to see the amazing things God has in store for us?

Be prepared, as the Scouts would say. But be prepared both practically and spiritually if you want to be an effective spiritual leader.

Questions for reflection

1. What particular practicable steps might I take to enhance my skills as a leader?
2. Joshua and the people rose 'early in the morning' to obey God's command. Am I a motivated self-starter or more laissez-faire in my approach?
3. Am I as concerned to give myself to spiritual preparation as to practical preparation in leadership?

6. Take risks (Joshua 3:6–17)

When I was a young pastor, I much admired a deacon in my church who held senior positions in business and in several Christian organizations as well. I learned a huge amount from him about leadership. I thought that everything he touched was successful. But some years later, when I had matured more, I discovered that not only had he experienced failure, but that he and other leaders knew that a certain amount of failure was inevitable and, consequently, even acceptable. That is because leadership involves taking risks. It is never safe.

When Joshua stood on the banks of the River Jordan with the whole of Israel watching him, he was taking a huge risk. He trusted God to part the river and make a dry path for the people to cross over to the other side. But what if God didn't do it? What if Joshua had made it all up? What if it was an experience doomed to fail? The consequences for Joshua's leadership would have been fatal, as verse 7 acknowledges in a backhanded way, and the consequences for the people would have been catastrophic.

Lee Iacocca, who served Ford and Chrysler as America's foremost automobile executive from the 1960s to 1980s, once said, 'If you take no risks, you do nothing.'[1] Joshua was not prepared to do nothing, and took the risk of visibly parading the ark of the covenant before the people as it went ahead of them to the river. He then told the priests, 'When you reach the edge of the Jordan's waters, go and stand in the river' (verse 8). The command was an act of faith that God would deliver on his word. Faith is not faith if all we do is act on what we can already be sure about, what we can already see.[2] Faith involves risk, and leadership involves risks, so Christian leaders have a double portion of risk to cope with in their lives. Joshua would have looked pretty silly if the waters had not parted. The result would have been not only failure to enter the Promised Land, but also a multitude of wet, muddy, priestly feet.

This does not excuse reckless decision-making, or mean that every risk is worth taking, or that every risk comes from God. There is wise and foolish risk-taking. Joshua's experience highlights some of the issues.

Risk and responsibility for others

In taking risks, the leader must be acutely aware of the impact that these will have on others. Joshua was very aware of the impact of his instructions on the people as a whole, and so is careful to explain to them:

- the basis for his decision ('Come here and listen to the words of the LORD your God');
- the reason why he thought his decision would prove right ('the living God is among you and . . . he will certainly drive out before you' the present occupants of the land); and

- the procedure they were to adopt in implementing it ('choose twelve men . . .').

By definition, it is impossible to ensure that all risks would pay off. But if they did, they would not be risks! Risks are about probabilities, not certainties, and inevitably expose us to the possibility of failure and even danger. That's why, in making decisions that implicate others, we need to be sure of our ground. Have we listened to God in this? What is the balance of probabilities? How important is it that we take this risk?

My great mentor Gilbert Kirby[3] took enormous risks in trusting younger people in leadership and giving them responsibility, including me. Sometimes people could see the obvious potential in the younger leaders he encouraged, and sometimes eyebrows were raised since others could see little or no potential. He was able to spot the gifts that lay buried in some young lives and help to uncover them so that others could appreciate them as well. Overwhelmingly, the risks he took paid off, and a whole generation of Christian leaders are in his debt as a result. But that's because he took the risks wisely. He would have been unwise to encourage those who were never going to make it in leadership. To promote people to places of responsibility and promise them a great future in leadership when they clearly don't have one causes damage to the individuals concerned, not least through disappointed expectations and a feeling that God has let them down. It probably also causes damage to others on whom they have clumsily practised their non-existent leadership skills. It can be like an untrained surgeon wielding a scalpel in an unsterilized operating theatre, something to be avoided at all costs!

There is a delicate balance to be struck between faith and fact. Any Christian leader should seek to operate by faith and not just by sight. Equally, they should want to raise the faith level among their followers so that they believe in the God who can, and does, do the impossible. Yet, at the same time, the leader needs to operate with pastoral sensitivity. Occasionally well-meaning leaders have encouraged prayer for healing (sometimes as a result of lacking a Christian view of death, but that's another story!) which has not happened, or encouraged words of prophecy which have not proved true. The effect on the weaker Christian who has believed and hoped in the truth of the promises can be devastating, even to the extent of giving up on following Jesus.

Take risks, but be aware of their impact on others.

Risk and one's own reputation

We saw in chapter 3 that one of the themes of Joshua is that God is concerned to enhance his status as a leader in the eyes of the people, 'so that they may know that I am with you as I was with Moses' (verse 7). Yet leaders should never be pre-occupied with their own reputation. As a friend used to say to me, 'The great thing about not having a reputation is that you can't lose it.' That's a nice thought, but an illusion as far as leadership goes, since having a reputation is really un-avoidable. Leaders gain reputations for wisdom, godliness, determination, faithfulness, passion, prayer, or for insecurity, egomania, recklessness, irresponsibility, or its opposite, an undue caution that means no change ever takes place.

Since we're not building our own empires, the only reason why reputation really matters is that the reputation of a Christian leader and God's reputation are inextricably linked. So Joshua's reputation is enhanced because he takes wise risks, the purpose of which is that the people might know that the living God is among them, as verse 10 says, and that eventually the surrounding nations might know that too. 'The point of exalting Joshua,' as Firth comments, 'is not to boost Joshua's ego, but rather that Israel might know Yahweh is present with him, demonstrating this to those who may be unsure. Joshua's status depends on Yahweh's initiative . . .',[4] not his self-promotion, nor on his public relations firm or management consultants! Having confidence in their leaders is crucial, and here God authenticates Joshua's leadership before the people.[5]

Insofar as our reputation and God's are intertwined, we should ask whether any risk we take will honour God or dishonour him in the eyes of others. Will the decision encourage others to believe, or will it jeopardize their faith? Will the risk promote the gospel or harm it? Having done that, we can leave our personal reputations in the hands of God, whose servants we are.

Risk and reward from God

The obvious outcome of this chapter is that when the people took the risk of standing in the Jordan, 'the water upstream stopped flowing. It piled up in a heap a great distance away . . . So the people crossed over opposite Jericho', with the priests standing in the middle of the river 'on dry ground' (verses 16–17). If they had not taken the risk, they would not have witnessed the miracle, nor benefited from its outcome. The 'amazing things' (verse 5) that God had promised them were occurring before their very eyes, and they were not merely spectators of them, but participants too.

What God was rewarding, of course, was not the fact that they took a risk just for the sake of taking one, but they took a risk that demonstrated obedience and trust in his word. Such risks pay rich rewards in revealing more to us of God's grace and salvation.

If you want to be a leader, you have to take risks, but take them wisely, knowing the cost involved to you and others, and even more to God, if they fail. Oh, and don't run away with the idea that all risks are great risks. Many are just ordinary, daily, routine risks involved in any relationship or decision-making. Kouzes and Posner understood that when they wrote that 'boldness [in other words, risk-taking] is not necessarily about go-for-broke, giant-leap projects. More often than not it's about starting small and gaining momentum . . . The most effective change processes are incremental, not one giant leap.'[6]

Be a wise risk-taker for God.

Questions for reflection

1. Where do I place myself on a scale of 1 to 10, where 1 represents someone who is risk averse and 10 represents a risk-taker?
2. How do I understand the relationship between taking risks and exercising faith in God?
3. What holds me back from taking risks? Are they wise or foolish, even sinful, restraints? Do the restraints mean I miss out on rich rewards in God's service?

7. Recall history (Joshua 4:1 – 5:12)

The passage across the Jordan was as successful as it was miraculous, but from the perspective of leadership, what happened next might appear to be something of an anti-climax. Joshua 4 – 5 is a complex passage, preoccupied with the placing of memorial stones and the reintroduction of the rites of circumcision and the Passover. It's perhaps not how we would have celebrated. Yet underneath, it has something important to say to leaders.

Unravelling the chapters

Stay with me a little as I map out the chapter before turning to the significance it has for leaders, since the one is connected with the other. Many see the chapters as a composite piece stitched together from different accounts. But, as Marten Woudstra comments, 'If the chief purpose of ch. 4, the erection of the memorial stones, is kept in mind, the apparent lack of order and of composition, which many have thought to characterize the account . . . ceases to be a pressing problem.'[1] Once they'd crossed the Jordan, Joshua commanded the people to remove the twelve stones from the middle of the river where the priests had stood with the ark, and 'put them down at the place where you stay tonight' (verse 3). This they did, setting them up at Gilgal (verse 19). The purpose was that they should provoke the next generation to ask questions about what they symbolized, just as today people continue to ask the meaning of stone circles like Stonehenge. The difference is that while we can only speculate about Stonehenge – and boy, do we speculate! – the message of these stones was abundantly clear:

> He said to the Israelites, 'In the future when your descendants ask their parents, "What do these stones mean?" tell them, "Israel crossed the Jordan on dry ground." For the LORD your God dried up the Jordan before you until you had crossed over. The LORD your God did to the Jordan what he had done to the Red Sea when he dried it up before us until we had crossed over. He did this so that all the peoples of the earth might know that the hand of the LORD is powerful and so that you might always fear the LORD your God.
> (4:21–24)

Talk of the original and the ultimate placement of the stones is interlaced with comments on how God strengthened Joshua's status as a leader (verse 14), how the river returned to normal when the priests came up out of it (verses 15–18), how surrounding kings quaked with fear at the news of Israel's advance (5:1), and the reintroduction of the covenant rite of circumcision and the Passover meal (5:2–12).

What does it all mean?

So what's the point? We might say that Joshua has given us a lesson in priorities, and that would be right. The people have crossed over into Canaan, and the first thing they do is set up memorial stones and engage in religious ceremonies. Surely they had parties to attend, plans to finalize, armies to organize, enemies to engage. Wasn't this a waste of time? Was this just delaying tactics to avoid the battle?

Absolutely not. These acts keep them focused on God. The stones would bear witness for generations to come that their act of crossing the Jordan was not of their own doing, but an act of God's powerful grace. The practice of circumcision had lain dormant during the wilderness years, and so those who crossed the Jordan had not been circumcised. Its revival at this point (5:4–9) was a resetting of the special covenant relationship that Israel had with God and a constant physical reminder to them that they belonged to him alone. Three days later they reintroduced the Passover meal (for which circumcision was needed), in order to celebrate their earlier great delivery from Egypt (5:10–12). Both of these signalled that a new day had dawned, Egypt was fully and finally behind them, and their relationship with God was restored. They were entering Canaan as God's elect people, not as a motley collection of disparate tribes who would sell their allegiance to anyone who paid sufficient for it. That's why these ceremonies were a priority.

The importance of telling the story

So what's the relevance of all this to leadership? Simply that both the placing of the memorial stones and the reintroduction of the rites and rituals are ways of vividly reminding the people of their story, and in so doing, of shaping their identity. Our past has a huge influence on our present. We may sometimes think of that in negative terms, since we all know people whose past experiences have damaged them, as maybe our own have done. But for the most part, remembering is a constructive, positive thing to do.

In his book *Leading Minds*, Howard Gardner, Professor of Cognition and Education at Harvard Graduate School, identified the ability to articulate the people's story as an important element in making leaders effective. He writes,

> Leaders achieve their effectiveness chiefly through the stories they relate . . . In addition to communicating stories, leaders *embody* those stories. That is, without necessarily relating their stories in so many words or in a string of elected symbols, leaders . . . convey their stories in the kinds of lives they themselves lead and, through example, seek to inspire others.[2]

That's exactly what Joshua did. He not only lived through the story of Israel's deliverance from Egypt and its dependence on God through the wilderness years, but continued to embody the story as they moved forwards to enter fully into God's promise of a land for them. He was one of the generation who had witnessed the miracle of the exodus, and alone, apart from Caleb, was spared to live long enough to witness the equally miraculous entry to the Promised Land. He embodied the story, too, in his attention to the written law and to the living voice of God. He embodied it – not perfectly, for no-one does – but admirably in the way he lived and led. Furthermore, he articulated the story in words on many occasions[3] and, as here, made use of the symbolic acts of circumcision and Passover to reinforce the message.

Leaders function at a number of levels – Howard Gardner distinguishes the way in which different levels of leaders tell the story in different ways:

- An *ordinary leader* 'by definition the most common one simply relates the story of his or her group as effectively as possible'. That covers most of us who are leaders.
- *Innovative leaders* reawaken a story. They 'take a story that has been latent in the population or among members of their chosen domain and bring new attention or a fresh twist to that story'. He cites Margaret Thatcher and Ronald Reagan as political leaders who did this.
- Then there are *visionary leaders* who are 'not content to relate a current story or reactivate a story, [but who] actually create a new story, one not known to most individuals before . . .'. Such leaders, Gardner comments, are very rare, and there are probably only one or two of them in any generation. Not surprisingly, Moses and Jesus are his foremost examples, with Gandhi also being named. If he were writing now, he'd probably include Nelson Mandela.[4]

It was Barack Obama's ability to tell, and even more embody, the story that got him elected as president of the USA. He not only personified the land of opportunity as a black man being elected to the highest political office in the nation, but he used his brilliant gift of oratory to craft the story. He captured it and the aspiration of the American people through the story of one woman, Ann Nixon Cooper, who was 106 years old and had cast her vote in Atlanta.

She was born just a generation past slavery; a time when there were no cars on the road or planes in the sky; when someone like her couldn't vote for two reasons – because she was a woman and because of the color of her skin.

And tonight, I think about all that she's seen throughout her century in America – the heartache and the hope; the struggle and the progress; the times we were told that we can't, and the people who pressed on with that American creed: Yes we can.

At a time when women's voices were silenced and their hopes dismissed, she lived to see them stand up and speak out and reach for the ballot. Yes we can.

When there was despair in the dust bowl and depression across the land, she saw a nation conquer fear itself with a New Deal, new jobs, a new sense of common purpose. Yes we can.

When the bombs fell on our harbor and tyranny threatened the world, she was there to witness a generation rise to greatness and a democracy was saved. Yes we can.

She was there for the buses in Montgomery, the hoses in Birmingham, a bridge in Selma, and a preacher from Atlanta who told a people that 'We Shall Overcome.' Yes we can.

A man touched down on the moon, a wall came down in Berlin, a world was connected by our own science and imagination.

And this year, in this election, she touched her finger to a screen, and cast her vote, because after 106 years in America, through the best of times and the darkest of hours, she knows how America can change.

Yes we can.

America, we have come so far. We have seen so much. But there is so much more to do. So tonight, let us ask ourselves – if our children should live to see the next century; if my daughters should be so lucky to live as long as Ann Nixon Cooper, what change will they see? What progress will we have made?

This is our chance to answer that call. This is our moment.[5]

That's telling the story of a nation and rejuvenating its identity at its best.

Leaders need to tell the story of their church or organization again and again, in order that they might not lose their identity or have their vision clouded. At a time when many think only the latest is the best, and we're removing the memorial plaques and symbols of yesteryear from our churches, we need to think of fresh ways to tell our stories and novel ways of recalling our history, or else we become rudderless and drift into being something we were never meant to be. The military services with their rituals, medals, remembrance occasions and the construction of new commemorative sites perhaps have a thing or two to teach the church in this regard. As a non-military person, I'm impressed at their ability to inspire loyalty and camaraderie, to rally people to the cause. There's much more to it than this, of course, but telling the story, in the multitude of ways they do, is a major factor in their exciting allegiance to a common vision. Articulating our story is what keeps us on track.

Joshua serves as our model in this regard, as he retells the story of the exodus and the crossing of the Jordan. Ours is a much greater story than his, and greater by far than the story of any one organization or church. It's a story of deliverance from sin, of the defeat of death, of victory over Satan, of freedom from condemnation and of reconciliation with God, through the death and resurrection of Jesus. Ours is a salvation that outshines any national story. We're nobodies who by grace have become the people of God. We've a hope of a renewed and restored creation in which God will reign supreme. That's a story worth telling.

As Asaph urged, in a lengthy psalm which sets out the story of Israel and reaches its climax in extolling the skilful leadership of David, we shouldn't hide the past from the next generation, but rather, 'will tell the next generation the praiseworthy deeds of the LORD'.[6] Israel knew the power of the story being told by the lips of the leader.

Don't bury the past. Know the past, study it and retell it in fresh ways in order that today's generation may be inspired by the power of our gospel and faithful to our living, ever-contemporary God.

Questions for reflection

1. What is my attitude to the story of the people I lead? Do I think their past history irrelevant and that everything began with my arrival as their leader?
2. How might I communicate the story of the past to inspire people in the present?
3. What sort of leader do I honestly aspire to be: ordinary, innovative or visionary?

8. Gain respect (Joshua 4:14)

God seems very intent on 'exalting' Joshua and encouraging the people to 'stand in awe of him all the days of his life, just as they had stood in awe of Moses' (verse 14), as we have already seen in passing. It's time now to look at this in its own right and to consider it a little more expansively.

By definition, leadership involves having people follow you. If no-one is following, then, clearly, you cannot be a leader. In fact, it has recently been argued that the concept of 'follower-ship' is far more significant than we have thought up to now, and should become central to our study and discussion about the nature of leadership, not least because it is changing the nature of contemporary leadership.[1] But Joshua's day was simpler, and our purpose is more straightforward. We ask, whom do people follow? They follow the people whom they respect.

Joshua had earned the people's respect before Moses had died, otherwise they would not have been content to trust him afterwards. They first explicitly voice their respect in 1:16, when Reuben, Gad and Manasseh pledge their loyalty and obedience to him. The honour he receives as Israel's leader crops up again in 3:7, and again here in 4:14. As time goes by, his fame spreads beyond the confines of Israel 'throughout the land' (6:27).

Receiving honour

The first thing to notice about this is that Joshua is not on an ego trip. He's not anxious about his image, or indulging in self-promotion, or protecting himself behind layers of insulating lackeys to give off signals of how important he is. He enjoys honour because it is the Lord who exalts him. Apart from the first reference to it in 1:16, the other references all clearly make God the subject of the sentence. 'The Lord said to Joshua, "I will begin to exalt you . . ."'; 'That day the Lord exalted Joshua . . .'; 'The Lord was with Joshua and his fame spread . . .' In his sovereign freedom, God chooses whom he wills to lead his people. It does not depend on what school they attended or what university education they had. It doesn't depend on a person's wealth, accent, family or connections. What counts is simply whether God has chosen, called and anointed them or not.

This is not to deny that there are many who seem to get into leadership positions in Christian circles apparently because of their social standing rather than their spiritual endowment. Sad to say, the church is often influenced by the world's way of thinking and working, where independent schooling and Oxbridge education, or sometimes simply muscle, are assumed to fit one for leadership. These might provide some natural advantages (as well as some liabilities), but Christians operate on a different set of criteria, and since everyone will have their work subjected to God's testing in the end, as mentioned in chapter 1, it's not for us to worry about them. Our ambition should be to ensure that we are in a position to be honoured by God for our leadership, whatever our background may be.

Human honours and praise are worth nothing.[2] Only the honour God gives will count for eternity.

The evangelical distortion

The evangelical church is often somewhat paranoid about personality cults (at least in theory), and with good reason. Other sections of the church claim to avoid the trap by being more concerned with the office than the person who occupies it. But in practice, neither those who are concerned about the office nor evangelicals who are more concerned with the person avoid the traps of the personality cult. Whatever their rhetoric or denials, evangelicals will often be enthusiastic groupies, whether it be of a modern musical, a worship leader, a charismatic miracle worker or an old-fashioned Bible expositor.

It is true that there are some people who see it as their mission to keep leaders humble and to puncture the slightest hint of any pride they might suspect. They sometimes even resort to rudeness as a means of doing so. (I have a few letters and emails to prove this!) Their attitudes sometimes mirror the widespread cultural suspicion of anyone who is in authority or leadership. So leadership can be a quite humbling place to be, and attacks and criticism, justified or otherwise, will certainly come. Therefore, leaders need to be secure persons in Christ, while at the same time eschewing arrogance and cultivating humility.

Scripture teaches us that it is right to show respect for one's leaders, as David did to Saul, who, for all his faults, was still 'the Lord's anointed'.[3] There are clear biblical commands about the need to respect one's leaders and honour them.

Paul's first letter to Timothy says that 'elders who direct the affairs of the church well are worthy of double honour'.[4] Hebrews 13:7 and 17 call on the church to honour their leaders and even to 'submit to their authority'. As well as thanking God for them, leaders deserve encouragement and appreciation for their abilities, qualities and achievements. But showing such honour falls far short of worshipping them.

Our respect for leaders, though, should be matched by a sense of caution, because our trust can never ultimately be in humans. They are only ever fallible human beings who may well falter or fail. Some failures, like moral ones in the financial or sexual realm, may be obvious. But there are other more subtle failures of pride, taking excess authority to oneself, power abuse, laziness, unbiblical or (even more commonly) sloppy teaching, cynicism, or the making of empty promises, which are not so obvious. The psalmist was wise to warn us, 'Do not put your trust in princes, in human beings, who cannot save.'[5] Many a younger leader has been disappointed when a well-established leader has failed, but they should not have been overawed by them in the first place. We have only one Teacher and one Lord.[6]

For all the cautions, however, leaders should be shown respect, especially where it is evident that God is honouring them. Joshua wasn't perfect, and we shall review some of his mistakes and shortcomings in the following chapters. But he was respected by the people, and rightly so, because God honoured him.

Earning respect

As well as being a gift from God, respect is something that is earned. But how do we earn it? There are several factors. Let me list a few.

Competence

This is most evident in Joshua. As a military leader, he demonstrated the qualities required of successful generals: courage,
strategic thinking, wise employment of resources, ability
to inspire the troops, knowledge of the enemy and, above
all, victory on the battlefield. The competences needed to
earn people's respect will depend on our particular field of
operations. But the generic skills of leadership that we are
considering in this book, such as the ability to shoulder responsibility, make wise decisions and plan ahead, are vital.

Some leaders either never gain respect or quickly lose it
because, quite frankly, they are incompetent. Others can see
that, even if the leaders cannot see it themselves.

Character

The question of character, addressed only in an implicit way
in Joshua, took centre stage in the New Testament's later
consideration of leadership. As he instructs Timothy and Titus
about who would make suitable elders, Paul majors on their
character rather than the tasks they will undertake.[7] They need
to be 'able to teach',[8] but otherwise it is about their self-
discipline, their temperate natures, personal maturity, ability
to handle money and their family. They need to be 'worthy of
full respect' and 'have a good reputation with outsiders'.

Most of this revolves around the quality of integrity or
authenticity that every leadership survey places high on the
list of people's expectations.[9] Integrity matters more than
intelligence.[10] Integrity means that every aspect of our lives is
in sync with every other aspect of our lives. Another way of
saying this is that personal 'credibility is the foundation
of leadership'.[11]

When General Norman Schwarzkopf Jr, who commanded
the Gulf War and removed the occupying forces of Iraq from

Kuwait, was asked about the essential qualities of courageous leadership, he replied,

> Character is the fundamental attribute of all great leaders. It's more important than anything else. Competence is important, certainly, but if you had to sacrifice one, you would give up competence before character. Character is everything.
>
> In times of crisis, when people must pick a leader from their peers, they always select the leader based on character.[12]

That is because in times of crisis, people must know they can trust their leaders.

Some leaders fail to earn the respect of others not because they are incompetent, but because they lack the character to put their competence to good use. This is often not due to some glaring failure in their lives. More often than not, it is because of a lack of personal maturity, emotional stability or inner strength. They lack the robust character that every leader needs and, intentionally or not, communicate signals of weakness, self-absorption, reserve, or that they are easily led and swayed. Alternatively, they are domineering and insensitively demanding. If the messenger isn't convincing, then the message won't be either.[13]

Relationships

Kouzes and Posner express a simple but essential truth when they write that *'Leadership is relationship.* Leadership is a relationship between those who aspire to lead and those who choose to follow. It's the quality of the relationship that matters most when we're engaged in getting extraordinary things done.'[14] Leaders establish respect by bonding with those who follow them. Social skills are vital for them to be able to persuade (not command in a peremptory fashion) others to follow them faithfully. Trust needs to develop rather than be assumed, and it will develop where leaders are genuinely more concerned about the people they are leading than their own reputations or agendas. Other ingredients of relationship building include the ability to listen, simple honest communication and transparent openness, including the admission of failure when necessary. Much leadership fails because it is viewed, rightly or wrongly, as a power play on behalf of the leader.

Gravitas

This is not to imply that leaders have to be serious people who can never relax and enjoy life. But it is to say that leaders need to be people of dignity who show they can be serious about issues when it counts, especially about gospel ministry and kingdom matters. Proverbs draws a startling picture of the fool, who is sometimes malicious but often just a sort of jester. Fools regularly show themselves up for what they are by being unable to discipline their temper or control their speech.[15] Ecclesiastes comments that putting fools in high positions and unsuitable people in powerful roles is not just stupidity but an evil.[16]

Perhaps there are no shortcuts to gaining gravitas. It is usually something that develops with experience. Some younger leaders have it from the start, and some older people never achieve it and never will, however long they live. But normally, younger leaders have to work at gaining respect simply because of their age. Paul hints that this was a problem for Timothy and something he had to work hard to overcome.[17] Paul's advice was that he should avoid fruitless quarrels, train himself in godliness, set an example 'in speech, in conduct, in love, in faith and in purity', keep clear priorities in preaching

Scripture, and work diligently and wholeheartedly.[18] That's still the best advice in developing leadership gravitas.

May God exalt you in your leadership, and may you gain the respect of those who follow you. But remember, you can't make anyone respect you unless God is in it. You can help to gain respect by working at your role, your life and your beliefs 'so that everyone may see your progress'.[19] Other than that, leave it to God.

Questions for reflection

1. What indications are there that people respect me as a leader? Do they merely tolerate or even humour me?
2. Am I in danger of seeking to build a personality cult rather than wanting honour to be given exclusively to God?
3. What steps can I take to earn greater respect and lessen any threats to that respect?

9. Surrender status (Joshua 5:13–15)

The greatest peril of Christian leadership is that we think too much of ourselves. We're obviously gifted and probably have something of a track record, or else we would not be trusted as a leader. Consequently, we can easily cross a line so that it is our plans, our strategies, our abilities, our status and our rights that become the most important thing to us.

It is perhaps no accident that Joshua encountered 'the commander of the army of the LORD' (verse 14) just at the time when God had exalted him in the eyes of others (4:14) and his leadership had been given a huge boost. Recent events would have made him very vulnerable to temptation, and here is a graphic lesson in guarding against it.

The question Joshua asks

When Joshua confronted the 'man standing in front of him with a drawn sword in his hand', his question to him was: 'Are you for us or for our enemies?' In some respects it's the obvious question to ask. Soldiers always want to know which side anyone approaching them is on. So do politicians. According to one of Margaret Thatcher's biographers, 'Is he one of us?' became one of the 'emblematic themes' of her premiership, and the question would be posed 'fiercely' about anyone before they were appointed to a post.[1] The truth is, it is a perennial question.

The question may be natural, and even at times necessary, but usually it is more of an expression of our not-yet-fully-redeemed natures than anything else. It is often a cloak for three besetting sins of leadership.

First, it may be an expression of personal pride

Joshua should perhaps be absolved from the charge of personal pride because his question does not ask are you for *me* but are you for *us*. He is acting as a leader in the interests of the people he leads. But it is easy to say 'us' and mean 'me' because what we're really concerned about is our own position and reputation.

A formidable preacher of an earlier generation, Alan Redpath, could be quite direct about such issues. Preaching on this passage, he once said, 'If any of you are seeking a position of power in your church, I hope you will resign – or get right with God. We need men of God, men who have been broken by the Spirit of God, men who desire only the glory of God in our churches today.'[2]

That's telling you! God uses people who are poor in spirit to lead his work, not those who are self-sufficient and confident in their own strength.[3]

Curiously, one way in which pride expresses itself is in terms of a competitive spirit, which is a special weakness of those who are insecure in their own skin and their own calling. The work of God is never dependent on one person and, through his Spirit, God always provides a multitude of people

JOSHUA 5:13–15 | 61

to lead it with differing gifts and personalities. The church benefits when they work together harmoniously, recognizing each other's skills, and suffers when personal envy or rivalry infects relationships.

Second, it may exhibit a spirit of divisive partisanship

We love to draw boundaries by which to include or exclude people. That was what Jesus' disciples did one day when they saw a man driving out demons in his name and told him to desist 'because he was not one of us'. Rather than congratulating them, Jesus rebuked the disciples for their overzealous and overprotective response, since anyone who did such a thing in Jesus' name would not be saying anything bad about him in the next breath. Jesus' verdict was: 'Whoever is not against us is for us.'[4] As James Edwards comments, 'This saying shows the Master to be more inclusive than his disciples. The making known of his name is more important than their distinctions (see Phil. 1:12–18).'[5] Just so.

But how does this tie up with the apparently opposite saying of Jesus that 'whoever is not with me is against me'?[6] One solution is to see that in the first case, where Jesus is inclusive, the disciples' problem was whether this man belonged to their group or not. Their concern was that the exorcist wasn't known to them and wasn't part of the group who gathered around Jesus. In the second case, where he is exclusive, the question was one of commitment to Jesus himself, 'where there can be no neutrality'.[7] The first cautions us not to be too dogmatic about the boundaries of our human cliques, especially in the church, whereas the second calls us to be uncompromising about the person of Jesus and his gospel.[8] While we must remain uncompromising about the gospel, we must be very careful to distinguish that from dividing the church on secondary grounds, such as personalities, cultural differences or attitudes to human plans. And that leads me to the third possible motive for Joshua asking the question.

Third, it might reveal a commitment to human plans, albeit unconsciously

On the verge of Jericho, Joshua is more than likely to have his plans for conquering the city in his mind. He wouldn't want a foe discovering them or a friend interfering with them at the last moment. Hence, perhaps, his question to the uninvited figure who stood before him.

Leaders need to be people who can create strategic plans for the future. Without these, groups just muddle along, usually achieving little. But once plans are conceived or adopted, they have a tendency to take over. Instead of serving us, they become our masters and we serve them. If the plan is our own, we can become very possessive of it. Most of us, however, adopt someone else's plan or method, often without giving sufficient thought as to whether it is appropriate to our situation or needs adapting in any way. We download it on people who often end up somewhat boxed in by it and no longer sensitive to the leading of God's Spirit.

The issue here is that we are in danger of making our plans the test of people's commitment and loyalty. Are they with us or against us? We must be careful to distinguish between loyalty to God and loyalty to our plans. They are not necessarily the same!

It is too easy to claim that God is on our side when greater humility might be appropriate. Good and godly members of leadership teams are quite capable of having different views about, say, mission strategy without that needing to be turned into a contest as to whose side God is on. Doris Goodwin in her brilliant biography of Abraham Lincoln records a comment of his when the Civil War was not going according to plan:

> 'In great contests,' he wrote in a fragment found among his pages, 'each party claims to act in accordance with the will of God. Both *may* be and one *must* be wrong. God cannot both be *for* and *against* the same thing at the same time. In the present civil war it is quite possible that God's purpose is something different from the purpose of either party,' and that God had willed 'that it shall not end yet.'[9]

Discussion, even disagreement, might be the way God leads his people to perceive a different, even greater plan, and to discover a greater unity than the laying down of a pre-determined plan by an enthusiastic leader who disregards the voice of others. Acts 15 perhaps serves as a wonderful model in this regard.

The answer Joshua receives

Joshua had been exalted by God in the eyes of the people, but this did not invest him with ultimate authority or put him in an untouchable place. Like Israel itself, there was a higher authority to whom he was subordinate. The one he encounters introduces himself as 'commander of the army of the LORD'. He certainly looked the part since he had a drawn sword in his hand. As commander, he was the one with the supreme military authority. But then, somewhat surprisingly, he tells Joshua to remove his sandals, as Moses was instructed to do at the burning bush,[10] because 'the place where you are standing is holy'.

Theologians speculate as to whether this was an angel or a pre-incarnate appearance of Jesus. He was evidently a messenger from God who combined the attributes of a divine warrior with priestly holiness. Theologians also speculate as to which army this man commanded. Was it the armies of Israel or the unseen armies of heaven?[11] But his exact identity, or the identity of the army, is a secondary issue compared with the visitor's mission. While the visitor does not answer Joshua's challenge – 'Are you for us or for our enemies?' – in words, his presence was sufficient to make clear that God was with him and the army of Israel would not be fighting alone and unaided. God and the unseen armies of heaven were on Israel's side and would give them victory. His mission, then, was both to provide Joshua with reassurance on the eve of battle and to keep him humble. The appearance of this commander was a gracious act of God to Joshua.

The response Joshua makes

Joshua's response is impressive. He does not argue, but shows humility by bowing face down to the ground, shows respect in calling the visitor 'my Lord', and shows obedience by taking off his shoes. Henry and Richard Blackaby may be right when they explain Joshua's response like this:

> A military man, Joshua immediately recognized one who carried greater authority than he . . . Joshua's military experience taught him to recognize authority. He knew subordinates did not argue with their superiors. The moment he recognized whose presence he was in, there was no wrestling, or arguing. There was only obedience.[12]

I am sure Joshua's military experience had a bearing on his response, but I am equally sure that his spiritual training was even more significant. His response revealed his heart. He wasn't in the business of leading in order to further his own name and reputation or boost his own status. He truly was both 'poor in spirit' and 'meek'.[13] So he immediately and willingly surrendered any status he had to the Lord who alone was in command, who alone could grant victory, and whose name and fame alone mattered.

Centuries later Jeremiah bluntly taught Baruch, his scribe, the same lesson when he was about to drown in self-pity. In the light of God's wider plans, Jeremiah challenged him, 'Should you then seek great things for yourself? Do not seek them.'[14]

We leaders perpetually need to be reminded of this. As I heard Ernest Clarke strikingly say when preaching on Naaman, 'Leadership is not about your position before people, but about your disposition before God.'[15] Those words should be burned into our hearts. Like Joshua, we need to surrender our concern with our own status to the Lord, since only when we do so will we be in a position to be useful to him.

Questions for reflection

1. Am I truly and completely surrendered to Christ?
2. Am I ever in danger of over-identifying my plans and programmes with God's?
3. How do I deal with the temptation to pride?

10. Trust God (Joshua 6:1–27)

Surely the strategy Joshua adopted for the conquest of Jericho was the most extraordinary and reckless one in military history, although Gideon's later defeat of the Midianites is perhaps comparable in its absurdity.[1] The thought that a fortified city like Jericho could be reduced to rubble and its inhabitants slaughtered (with the exception of Rahab's family) by a group of inexperienced nomads marching around it for seven days, while blowing trumpets and carrying their sacred cultic symbol, was nothing short of idiotic insanity. Yet that is exactly what happened.

The whole incident depends on verses 2 and 6: 'Then the LORD said to Joshua . . .', which is followed by 'So Joshua . . .' The great downfall of humanity had taken place because the snake asked Eve, 'Did God really say . . . ?'[2] Eve replied to the snake correctly, but did not then take her stand on what God had said, believing instead the lie the tempter had put in front of her. But Joshua acts differently. When God speaks, he trusts and obeys. The way the story is recorded emphasizes the simplicity of it all. 'The LORD said', 'so' Joshua did. No ifs or buts.

This chapter primarily records how God gave them the astonishing victory over Jericho because he was present among them. The ark of the covenant, which they carried around with them, served as his throne and was a visible signal that he was with them. And that is the crucial lesson here. As Dale Ralph Davis comments, the episode 'stresses how central Yahweh's presence is and how passive God's people are . . . Sometimes, it seems, God insists on by-passing his people's activity in order to enhance his own glory among his people'.[3]

Joshua shows himself to be a man of faith, which John White defined as 'man's response to God's initiative'.[4] It is a classic example of how believers can 'do business' beyond what seems reasonable in this world, 'and bring to pass otherwise unrealizable dreams'.[5] Even so, although it may be of secondary importance, woven unmistakably through the account of the conquest of Jericho, Joshua's qualities as a godly leader are clearly evident. Look at what it tells us about him.

His ear was tuned to God

No doubt Joshua was subject to a variety of voices and pressures, but only one really mattered to him. Above the cackle of other voices, he could clearly hear God's directing him. Listening to God is not the only thing a leader has to do, but it takes precedence over all others. Making time and space to listen to him and hear his direction and will is important for any leader, but is, alas, often squeezed out by the tyranny of busyness and engagements or the pressure of other voices telling them to do things this way or that.

His communication is inspiring

Having heard from God, Joshua immediately communicates what he has said to the priests and the army, at least sufficiently for the process of this strange warfare to begin. We have already discovered that Joshua was a skilful and inspiring communicator, and Jericho is yet a further example of this. He doesn't tell them they'll be marching round the walls thirteen times in all; he simply tells them to 'Advance!', without shouting but with trumpeters serving as the ancient equivalent of 'outriders'. Perhaps if he had told them the whole plan, they would have refused to take part. He knows just how much they needed to know, and that is what he tells them. So advance they do. Inspiring communication is a vital component of all ministry, and here, as elsewhere, Joshua uses his skill to maximum effect.

His obedience was faultless

As we saw above, he acted on God's word, getting the army to march around Jericho, and he did so without delay: 'Joshua got up early the next morning' (verse 12). There was no way he was going to drag his feet or reluctantly obey his Lord. Not for the first or last time he showed a readiness, indeed eagerness, to conform to his Lord's commands.

His stance was patient

The whole process went on for a week. When he was the UK Prime Minister, Harold Wilson is reported as saying that a week is a long time in politics. Events change very quickly. The week in Jericho must have seemed even longer than one in Westminster, but for the opposite reason. All week they trudged around Jericho, blowing their trumpets and carrying the ark, and nothing happened. The walls remained standing, the city went on functioning and no-one capitulated to the Israelites. One can imagine the inhabitants of Jericho scratching their heads at such strange behaviour, in both bewilderment and disbelief. Were Joshua's soldiers also growing sceptical? Was anything going to happen? Did they view the command to march around the city seven times on the seventh day as a measure of Joshua's own increasing desperation, or did they latch on to the significance of 'seven'? Whatever the attitude of others, Joshua seems to have been unwavering. He quietly persisted in trusting God when the evidence seemed stacked against him. Leaders need to be in the job for the long haul, not the quick fix. We're sometimes too impatient to see God do things according to our timetables and satisfy our demands when we want him to, rather than patiently trusting him.

His integrity was maintained

When the wall fell, Joshua immediately commanded 'the two men who had spied out the land' (verse 22) to go and rescue Rahab and her family. Even in the moment of victory he was not too busy to follow through on his commitment to a Gentile family. Some might have thought that was unimportant. Others might have said they felt no obligation to keep their promise made before the battle as a necessary step in counter-intelligence. Rahab and her family could have been treated as expendable, unfortunate casualties of war. But Joshua neither forgot his word, nor went back on his promise. In following through, he was perhaps unwittingly serving the greater purposes of God for Israel to be a blessing to all nations and for the inclusion of the Gentiles within the family of God. Joshua's life was marked by integrity through and through.

His faith was rewarded

As a result of their trust in God, Joshua and the people reaped a rich reward. Jericho was destroyed, a major obstacle had been removed and a major route into the Promised Land was secured. Joshua's own reputation was enhanced further, since people knew 'the LORD was with Joshua' (verse 27). Above all, the name and reputation of the God of Israel himself was magnified.

Jericho, as David Firth comments, is 'an exercise in trusting God, believing that if he had promised and was present, they would indeed receive the promise'.[6] And he concludes, 'This, then, is a powerful story. It offers us a battle plan that is so bizarre that no-one in his or her right mind would follow it – unless, of course, it was an opportunity to obey Yahweh. Then, of course, it does make sense, since the foolishness of God is wiser than the wisdom of the world.'[7]

Before Mary said the words to the servants at the wedding in Cana, Joshua knew the wisdom of the command to 'do whatever he tells you'.[8]

Questions for reflection

1. Is my ear tuned to God's voice both for the big decisions and the trivial tasks that make up the work of the leader?
2. How easy do I find it to trust God, especially when his word seems strange?
3. Am I impatient? Do I need to cultivate the spiritual discipline of waiting for God?

11. Face failure (Joshua 7:1–9)

From the heady heights of winning the battle of Jericho, Israel came crashing down as it experienced a rout at the battle of Ai. It is not an unknown pattern that great victories are followed by tragic defeats. One of the times when Christian leaders need to be most alert is when they have enjoyed a time of great blessing and fruitfulness. It is easy then, as here, to take one's eye off God and fail to keep humbly obeying him.

Failures happen. Since we have not yet reached perfection and since we are yet to be fully redeemed, failures will be part of our experience too. The issue here is how we deal with those failures and what we learn from them.

Crucible experiences

The value of what has come to be called crucible experiences has been much appreciated in contemporary discussions of business leadership. Warren Bennis and Robert Thomas, chief exponents of the concept, made the discovery after interviewing '40 top leaders in business and the public sector' and discovering that all of them, no matter what their age, 'were able to point to intense, often traumatic, always unplanned experience that had transformed them'.[1] They termed such negative tests and trials 'crucibles', 'after the vessels medieval alchemists used in their attempts to turn base metals into gold'. Crucible experiences are negative experiences that lead to

> a point of deep self-reflection that forced [the leaders] to question who they were and what mattered to them. It required them to examine their values, question their assumptions, hone their judgment. And, invariably, they emerged from the crucible stronger and more sure of themselves and their purpose – changed in some fundamental way.[2]

Joshua's crucible experience

Bennis and Thomas could have been writing about Joshua and the failure of Ai. The report begins with the conclusion: 'The Israelites were unfaithful . . . so the LORD's anger burned against Israel' (verse 1). Four elements emerge that tell us a little of what lay behind this and what steps Joshua took immediately when he confronted it.

First, they appeared to act wisely (verse 2)
They did their homework and sent out spies, as they had done before, to understand the size of the opposition, and then they took the scouts' report seriously. They did not engage in the battle without being aware of what they were up against, but rightly sought intelligence before making a move. So far, so good. Perhaps . . .

But second, they presumed on easy success (verses 3–4)
On the surface they presumed the battle would be easy because the spies reported that it would be. Large numbers of troops

weren't needed – two or three thousand would suffice – so there was no need to waste the energies of the rest of the army, they said. And that's what they did. Underneath this spoken reason for using a small army, however, there probably lies an unspoken, even unconscious, reason why they acted as they did. They were guilty of the sin of presumption. They presumed that God would be with them and would, of course, give them victory. Unusually, at the start of the Ai episode we read nothing of the Lord giving instructions about the battle or about Joshua listening to God's voice. Had not God given them victory at Jericho? Would he not also give them victory at Ai? Had he not promised to be with them? What, therefore, could hold them back? They had become confident in themselves rather than in the Lord.

Past blessings should never lead us to assume God's blessing in the present or in the future. Past victories should never lead us to assume that we will win another victory today, or tomorrow. Past growth should never lead us to assume that such growth will continue. Christian history is littered with churches, institutions and sites where the blessing of God was once powerfully at work but, alas, is no longer so. The buildings are often empty shells and the organizations shadows of their former selves. They stand as testimonies to what God once did but does not do any more.[3] Some of the people God has powerfully used in the past become presumptuous and do not continue to serve God faithfully. Some drop out of the scene altogether, while others continue to build their own empires. But God is not with them.

The presence and blessing of God has to be sought repeatedly and freshly throughout one's leadership. We cannot rely on it because of an initial calling, powerful spiritual experiences or dramatic visions in some time past. As sovereign Lord, his presence is in his gift alone; it is not our possession.

It is often when we are sailing along quite happily that the unexpected crucible experience happens, as it did at Ai.

Third, they were bewildered at their failure (verses 4–8)

When they were defeated at Ai, with a relatively modest number of casualties, they responded with a range of emotions, all of which were expressions of perplexity. The people were desperately afraid. Joshua and the elders were deeply remorseful, as was apparent because Joshua prostrated himself before God, and he and the elders tore their clothes and sprinkled dust on their heads, all signs of grief and sorrow. Joshua voices his bafflement at what had happened. In doing so, he says all the things we would typically say when faced with such a puzzle. Lord, he asks in contemporary language, what are you playing at? If you had intended to destroy us, you could have done that in Egypt; why bring us here to do so? Then he plays the 'if only' card, which is one of the most common cards we play in such circumstances. As he continues robustly voicing his bewilderment to God, he begins to get a right handle on the situation, as we'll shortly see.

Before we do so, we should note that the servants of God throughout the Old Testament are not afraid to raise their questions with God and ask him for an explanation of his actions. From within the experience of being assaulted, the psalmist encourages us:

> Trust in him at all times, you people;
>> pour out your hearts to him,
>> for God is our refuge.[4]

The Old Testament saints see no conflict between their questioning and their worship. They may voice their struggles with barely restrained passion, but they always do so within the context of knowing that God is sovereign. They simply want to penetrate his mysterious ways a little more so that their service to him might be all the more authentic. God is not answerable to them, any more than he is answerable to us. But he often accepts their interrogations and even graciously accommodates their human frailties by revealing something more of his purposes. We should never be afraid to express our struggles to God, even robustly. Indeed, what is the point of hiding them, since he knows our innermost thoughts anyway? To express them, to pour them out, is far healthier than to suppress them.

Fourth, Joshua focused on the right issue (verses 8–9)

As Joshua expressed his anguish to God, so he came to realize that the most important issue was not what had happened to them, but what their defeat would do to God's reputation. Other nations, he surmised, would gain confidence from their downfall and attack them and 'wipe out our name from the earth' (verse 9). The awful consequence of such a defeat would be that God's 'own great name' would be held in contempt, and not only would the Israelite people be extinguished, but the God whom they claimed as their protector would also be cast into oblivion. The issue, as Joshua comes to realize through prayer, is not how the failure reflected on them, but how it reflected on him.

Prayer works like that, doesn't it? We start off complaining to God about our struggles, and our horizons are filled with our own problems and disappointments, but as we talk with the Lord God of the universe, so we come to see how really very unimportant they are compared with the honour of his name and the need to live in accordance with his will. More than once I have come to realize that when I complain to God about this person or that situation, I hear the voice of God telling me to forgive or to leave the situation in his hands. The reputation that really matters is his, and the battle is also his.

Joshua begins by blaming God because he fails to realize that the problem is not with God but with the people. Yet, as Joshua pours out his heart, he encounters a God who, while not unfeeling, provides a true, if uncomfortable, diagnosis for their ills. The tearful voice of Joshua gives way to the majestic voice of God himself, which is the first step on the road to recovery and to putting the tragedy of Ai to rights.

Learning from crucible experiences

All leaders experience failures. I've known many a student who thinks they are going to be the exception, but they are unerringly mistaken. Sometimes the failures are our own fault; sometimes the fault lies with others. Sometimes failures are the result of circumstances, and sometimes we just don't know why they happen. The important thing then is to discover what we can learn from them and how to handle them. God uses failures for our good and for his own glory.

The value of crucible experiences, as mentioned above, is that they hone our judgments. They teach us not to make assumptions, to consult all those who are significant players in a decision, and to question things from a number of angles, not just one. They slow us down and teach us by hard experience not to come to premature judgments.

They also teach us to adapt, rather than just repeating the same old, same old, all the time. What works at one time or in one situation doesn't in another. There are no formulae that automatically guarantee success. To claim that leaders can always be proactive is a pipe dream. There are times when circumstances require leaders to be responsive and reactive. It is then that the skills of adaptation are necessary so that we still lead people forwards.

Hardships in leadership will enable us to develop hardiness in leadership. 'Hardiness' is the word used by Bennis and Thomas. They write, 'Hardiness is just what it sounds like – the perseverance and toughness that enable people to emerge from devastating circumstances without losing hope.'[5] It's easy to lead when all is going well. The quality of leadership is tested when things go wrong and failures occur. Can we keep going when the storms cause devastation, or only when the sun shines?

We can emerge from crucible experiences 'stronger and more secure in ourselves and of our purpose'.[6] More significantly, we can emerge from crucible experiences with a firmer trust in God, a greater understanding of his sovereignty, and a deeper grasp of his grace.

James put it neatly:

> Consider it pure joy, my brothers and sisters, whenever you
> face trials of many kinds, because you know that the testing
> of your faith produces perseverance. Let perseverance finish
> its work so that you may be mature and complete, not lacking
> anything. If any of you lacks wisdom, you should ask God,
> who gives generously to all without finding fault, and it will
> be given to you.[7]

When failures happen, keep going. But learn from them and be positively transformed by them. Aim for maturity. Find security in God. Pick yourself up in the strength of the Lord, and get going again for the sake of the people you lead.

Questions for reflection

1. Can I identify crucible experiences in my life? How did they change me?
2. As I reflect on failures, how could I have handled those situations differently?
3. What wisdom does Joshua give me for when things go wrong?

12. Confront sin (Joshua 7:10–26)

We come to one of the most delicate responsibilities of Christian leadership. Christian leaders are sometimes required to confront sin.

Having asked God why he had permitted Israel to be so roundly defeated at Ai, Joshua learned the reason: 'Israel has sinned; they have violated my covenant, which I commanded them to keep. They have taken some of the devoted things . . . they have put them with their own possessions. That is why the Israelites cannot stand against their enemies' (verses 11–12). Sin among the people had caused God to withdraw his blessing, and without his blessing they were nothing.

The example of Joshua

This painful episode in Israel's history does not say all that needs to be said about dealing with sin among God's people, but it gives us a start, and, to that extent, Joshua serves as a model of godly leadership.

First, Joshua acted at God's command (verses 10–13)

The first thing God said to Joshua was that he needed to 'stand up' and stop grovelling down on the ground. Their defeat had a cause, and something could be done about it. It was Joshua's responsibility as Israel's leader to take the necessary action. There is a place for the wringing of hands and the wailing of lament, but there comes a moment when it is right to stop just saying sorry and do something to transform the situation. Joshua had reached that moment.

The second step Joshua had to take, after standing up, was to 'consecrate the people', a phrase we've met before,[1] which meant the people undertook certain rituals and abstained from certain actions so as to recommit themselves to being God's special people, belonging to him alone. Before they could face the outcome of the investigation into who had sinned, they needed to be reminded of their identity as a chosen people.

The third step was to initiate the process by which the culprit who had brought such grief on Israel was to be identified. The day after their renewed consecration, the people presented themselves to Joshua in the presence of the Lord and underwent a process of elimination until the finger was pointed at Achan. Achan at least had the grace to admit his guilt and spare Israel further heartache. We do not know what method the Lord used to inform Joshua as to who was innocent and who was guilty. But Achan's immediate confession proved that it was reliable.

Second, Joshua handled the investigation wisely (verses 14–23)

Many preachers who are hot against sin are good at condemning whole congregations for wrongdoing, like school teachers who punish a whole class for the misdemeanour of one pupil. By the grace of God, Joshua avoids this. He does not blame everyone for the failure of one man. He deals directly and personally with the culprit and his family, rather than bringing everyone under condemnation and ratcheting up widespread guilt feelings.

It is true that Achan's family are condemned along with him, but there are probably several reasons for this. Today we see ourselves as individuals, but in ancient times people saw themselves essentially as belonging to others rather than as separate persons or in isolation. They understood collective solidarity and collective responsibility in a way we don't, at least in the Western world. Then, it was very unlikely that Achan could have acted alone without the knowledge of his family, and so they were complicit in his guilt. The consequences of sin are never confined to the one who commits it. Moreover, Achan's sin brought trouble on the whole of Israel, so removing such contamination from their midst leads to his whole family being expunged from the nation. Besides this, it serves to underline that Achan's disobedience was a terrible affront to God's holiness.[2]

Before acting further, Joshua ensured he had corroborating evidence of Achan's guilt. He sends people to find the banned goods that Achan had stolen as proof of his guilt. He does not operate on rumour or hearsay, and does not condemn before checking the facts. Churches can be frenetic rumour factories, and the sins of others can easily be magnified under the pretence of wishing to protect the purity of the church or the name of God. In dealing with people's sins, we are best to follow Joshua's example of talking with people directly, without presuming guilt, and seeking always to base our judgment on evidence rather than supposition or gossip.

Third, Joshua exercises painful discipline (verses 24–26)
When the guilt is proved, Joshua does not shirk his responsibility to exercise discipline, however painful it might be.

Given the time and cultural context in which this incident occurred, the punishment was death. In this way, the curse that afflicted the whole of the nation was removed. No leader today is called upon to exercise this kind of discipline. Under the new covenant, different forms of discipline are appropriate, as we will shortly explore. But while we are not called upon to exercise such punishments, we may well still be required to exercise discipline in the Lord's name, and we must have the courage to do so.

Confronting sin in the New Testament and beyond

Some examples

It was no light thing when Ananias and Sapphira sought to deceive the apostles in the early days of the church.[3] When confronting them, Peter made it plain that their sin was, in fact, against the Holy Spirit, that is, against God himself, not just an offence against, or an inconvenience to, human leaders. Their instant deaths dramatically portrayed the seriousness of their sin. It was, perhaps, a necessary way of establishing the importance of the high moral standards expected of God's fledgling church. But it is also the only example in the New Testament of such Old Testament punishments being experienced. From then on, sin in the church is taken seriously but dealt with differently. Peter may have warned Simon the former sorcerer with dire consequences, but it had the desired effect of leading him to repentance.[4]

Paul instructs the church at Corinth about the person practising incest to 'hand this man over to Satan for the destruction of the flesh, so that his spirit may be saved on the day of the Lord'.[5] But in doing so, it was clear that they were not to take the law into their own hands, but leave this person in the hands of God. Recalcitrant sinners seem mostly to have been expelled from the Christian community rather than suffering in other ways.[6] Although Paul could exercise strong leadership, he was aware of the need for the church never to overstep the mark in dealing with sinners so that they became overwhelmed by 'excessive sorrow', and to minister forgiveness and comfort, which was, after all, at the heart of the gospel.[7] Paul's 'rod of discipline', which he was not afraid to use in confronting a range of sins like greed, dishonesty, idolatry and arrogance (not just sexual immorality), normally seems to have taken the form of verbal rebuke or gentle pleading.[8] Paul seems to have been a great practitioner of Proverbs 27:5: 'Better is open rebuke than hidden love.'

The purpose of confronting sin

Jesus makes it abundantly clear that among his disciples the purpose of confronting anyone with their sin is to lead them to repentance and restoration, and to set free those who have erred. Having stressed the seriousness of sin,[9] Jesus turns to how to deal with it in the church.[10] He instructs his disciples to deal with it face to face, just as Joshua did, and to keep it as small and contained as they can. They must be especially careful not to spread chatter about someone's possible falling into sin under the guise of being spiritually concerned. One writer about church discipline complains, 'Unknown to me, a group once spent weeks praying about sins they felt I was guilty of. I had been prayer-gossiped, prayer-judged and prayer-condemned, long before I was approached.'[11] Clearly, his supposedly 'spiritual' brothers and sisters had not read the words of Jesus!

It is never right to begin by making the sin public, but always right to try to resolve the failure personally and to involve only 'one or two others' if that is unsuccessful. No premature judgments should be reached, but the evidence should be considered. In Jesus' teaching it is the evidence of 'two or three witnesses', as the law required,[12] rather than 'your word against his or hers'. In Joshua's case the evidence took the form of discovering the contraband rather than the testimony of witnesses, but the principle is the same. Only if all attempts at repentance, reconciliation and restoration on the small scale have failed should the church be informed. If stubborn refusal to recognize the error of their ways and amend them persists, then offenders should be treated as 'a pagan or a tax collector'.

Ways of confronting sin

Jesus' teaching and Paul's practice make it abundantly clear that there should be no rush to judgment. While the confronting of sin may be necessary, the Christian leader must always act with gentleness and humility, being aware of their own vulnerability: 'If someone is caught in a sin, you who live by the Spirit should restore that person gently. But watch yourselves, or you also may be tempted.'[13] 'If you think you are standing firm, be careful that you don't fall!'[14]

Furthermore, those who confront the sin of others should be careful not to magnify the failure, make more of it than is warranted or broadcast it to others. Love, remember, 'does not dishonour others . . . it keeps no record of wrongs . . . does not rejoice in evil . . . It always protects, always trusts, always hopes, always perseveres'.[15]

Sin does need to be confronted, since it may be a blockage in the channel of God's blessing, and removing the blockage can release blessing. A young friend of mine in the early days of his first ministry became aware that his church treasurer was committing adultery. It was the talk of the town; he didn't have to go searching for it. So, being new to ministry, he wisely took advice from those who were more experienced, but then confronted the man personally with his sin. The man did not react well. First of all he blustered, then boasted, and finally bullied. He was the person who wrote the cheques, he said, by which he meant that he was the one who gave the money that kept the church open and paid the pastor. Without his financial backing, the church would close. It depended on him. When that didn't work, he resorted to violence, punching my friend. But my friend held his nerve and gently but firmly insisted on the man's resignation, which he eventually received. Some time after this, my friend showed me a financial graph on the wall of his church. It showed that the church's giving took off the moment the old church treasurer resigned. The blockage to blessing had been removed. Years later they built a new church and now have a larger, healthier and more vibrant community in Christ than ever in their previous history.

So church leaders need to confront sin. But they put themselves on a dangerous path when they do, with many pitfalls and potential traps. Healthy discipline can too easily become a vehicle for control, pride, arrogance and the abuse of power. Distorted, it can become monstrous. 'But the abuses of discipline, rather than discipline itself, are what we must fear', and the absence of it 'will be incalculably greater' than its dangers.[16] Leaders need to go down the path cautiously, humbly, listening carefully to the Lord, applying the spiritual principles we have mentioned, and with the support of fellow leaders, remembering that ours is a gospel of grace and restoration. The purpose of confronting sin, wherever possible, is restoration in Christ.

Questions for reflection

1. Is my natural character one that relishes confrontation or avoids it? What implications does that have for my leadership?
2. Am I committed to total obedience to Christ in my own life and in the lives of those I lead?
3. How do I handle the failures of others? Do I make more or less of them than I should? Can I exercise discipline wisely?

13. Re-energize people (Joshua 8:1–29)

One of the most difficult challenges any leader can face is to inspire a people to advance again when they have just faced a debilitating setback. After the defeat at Ai, it's likely that Israelite morale was low and insecurities high. No doubt some would have voiced those familiar words: 'We've tried that before and it didn't work.' Joshua has a difficult task to persuade the people to pick themselves up and get going once more. Raising morale, renewing vision and re-energizing people after the stuffing has been knocked out of them are all part of the leader's job.

Joshua performs the task admirably. But how?

Joshua listens to God (verses 1–2)

Before he instils fresh energy into others, he needs to be re-invigorated himself for the task, and this he does by listening to God.

First, Joshua accepts God's encouragement

The words that he had often heard from God before now become particularly significant in view of the circumstances: 'Do not be afraid; do not be discouraged.' A temporary reversal does not spell an irreversible failure. God had not withdrawn his promise, nor changed his plan. In fact, what had happened was confirmation of the covenant agreement he had made with the Israelites: God's blessing depended on their obedience, so when Achan disobeyed him, his blessing was temporarily withdrawn. It may have been a sign of God's severity, but it was in fact a severe mercy, since he taught them a lesson in this relatively gentle way by a tragic, but limited, loss of life at Ai, and by punishing only the one responsible for the defeat together with his family. Having exercised his discipline and received his people's repentance, there was no need for the people to hold back but rather advance again. It was an example of the truth Hebrews was later to teach: discipline is a mark of love and relationship, and God exercises it 'for our good, in order that we may share in his holiness'.[1]

Furthermore, in case Joshua is hesitant, God assures him, 'I have delivered into your hands the king of Ai.' You can't get much clearer than that.

Discouraged leaders are unlikely to be able to inspire others. Whatever words may come out of their lips, the weariness, the downcast tone, the drooping shoulders and the unintended sighs are likely to communicate to others the discouragement they feel. God knows this and encourages Joshua first, in order that he might encourage others.

Second, Joshua obeys God's instructions

God commands him to take 'the whole army with you, and go up and attack Ai'. And that is what he does, taking 30,000 troops with him instead of the 3,000 who made up the earlier army.[2]

The command to take the whole army was both an extraordinarily gracious, and also a wise, move on God's part. He could have ensured victory over Ai with just a small fighting force, just as he was to do later when Gideon defeated the Midianities.[3] His power was not weakened as a result of their disobedience. However, in instructing the whole army to go up, God was being sensitive to the Israelites and not asking them to take a risk that, in view of the recent defeat, might have stretched their faith too far. They were not being instructed to venture into the battle in a foolhardy manner. By directing the whole army to go up, God was also teaching them that although he is the God of the miraculous and has power to do as he wills, he usually works through the ordinary, and by encouraging his people to use the means he has put at their disposal rather than rely on the easy supernatural option.

Joshua is marked by fresh obedience.

Third, Joshua adopts the Lord's plan

The strategy Joshua was instructed to adopt was not an outright attack, but to 'set an ambush behind the city'. It was to be taken by subterfuge. The Israelites were to advance on the city, and at the first sign of the army of Ai attacking them, they were to appear to be running away. With Ai's army pursuing them, the city itself would be left exposed and undefended. The hidden Israelites were then to enter it and destroy it.

No doubt there could have been alternative military plans, and, in all probability, the strengths and weaknesses of God's plan would have been discussed and evaluated by Joshua's colleagues. But Joshua simply obeys the Lord.

Joshua leads by example (verses 3–35)

Listening to God is a vital first step in re-energizing a discouraged people and preparing them to fight again. But that is only one blade, as it were, in the pair of scissors. The other blade is equally necessary if the scissors are to achieve their objective and cut Ai down to size! What completes this pair of scissors are Joshua's personal leadership skills. People who hear God's voice clearly can often be lovely, pious people, but they are not always effective in leading others. Ideally, both the gift of listening to God and of leading his people belong together, but they do not always do so. In such a situation, working with others in a cooperative way is vital. Piety alone is not enough to re-inspire and re-energize a discouraged people.

Here we can see four necessary attributes of a leader who wishes to inspire others.

First, Joshua engages in careful communication (verses 3–8)

Here is yet another example of Joshua's skill in communication. Having received the plan of attack from God, he now faithfully relays it to the people and takes them through it step by step. He encourages them to 'listen carefully' and, while making it clear that the plan comes from God, he is not afraid to say authoritatively, 'You have *my* orders.'

I was once told that if I failed to get my governing body to agree to something I wanted, it was because I had not communicated it adequately to them. I am not sure it's quite that simple. Sometimes it is the providence of God that leads a board to reach a different decision from the one you would like. But even if there are exceptions, the statement generally holds true. I have heard of many church meetings that have rejected their pastor's vision and plans because they have not been adequately explained, or because insufficient time was permitted for people to grasp them. Leaders can forget how long they took discussing and processing things before they came to a decision. It's good to recognize that others may need some time to think and pray things through too. Not everything has to be done yesterday! I know that, ironically, some of those churches that have rejected plans have done so not because they were against them – indeed, they have shared the vision and even had sympathy for the plan – but because they felt they were being railroaded into agreeing with them.

If people are to be inspired, communication matters.

Second, Joshua identifies with his people (verse 9)

Exactly who 'the people' mentioned in verse 9 are has been a cause of some confusion. Was it the army, as verse 13 suggests, or the non-fighting population, as a plain reading of the words might indicate? From our viewpoint, it doesn't make too much difference because the essential point remains true, whoever 'the people' were. Joshua does not withdraw to the security of his own tent, distanced from others. He shares their experience with them, whether it is the fears and un-certainties of the families left behind or the nerves and tensions of the forces preparing to attack.

Anthony King and Ivor Crewe have written a brilliant analysis of why governments blunder so badly in some of the policies and laws they attempt to adopt. One of the five main reasons they identify – and we'll look at another below – is because of what they call a cultural disconnect between the lives of the politicians and those of the people. They provide numerous examples of what they call a 'potentially virulent' disease, and argue that politicians need to be conscious of 'the utterly different lifestyles, tastes and preoccupations' they have from those of the electorate.[4] Steps have to be taken to minimize the disconnect, as Joshua does on the eve of the battle of Ai.

Inspiring leaders are never above others or disconnected from the people they lead, but share their fears and hopes, experiences and expectations, identifying with them as much as they can.

Third, Joshua marches in front of his army (verse 10)

Joshua did not march before them when Ai was first attacked, but now he sees the vital importance not only of sharing the hours before the battle with them, but of visibly leading them into battle himself. There was no better way to restore the morale of his dispirited army and reignite their confidence than by putting himself at their head and in the firing line. He would not have been able to instil fresh courage in them if he had remained in protected isolation watching them from afar. He needed to demonstrate the courage of his convictions.

King and Crewe identify the failure to do this as another of the key reasons why governments blunder. There is 'cultural disconnect', but 'operational disconnect' is also a cause of failure. This occurs when there is a gap between policy and implementation, theory and practice, idea and reality. They comment,

> It is an old maxim that anyone planning a military operation should ideally be put in charge of it – and should know in advance that he is going to be put in charge of it. Joining planning and operations in this way means that the individual in charge is playing for high stakes. He owns the operation. If he succeeds, he stands to be decorated and promoted. If he fails, he alone takes the blame.[5]

They comment that the generals of the Second World War are said to have been more successful than those of the First, 'because they were closer to the front line. The age of "château generalship" was over.'[6]

People soon come to suspect the authenticity of pastors who want their people to evangelize but never do so themselves, or urge their people to pray but are always absent from the prayer meeting, or who stress the importance of Scripture but whose preaching only ever lightly brushes with it. Such leaders do not galvanize others into action. Operational disconnect usually leads to operational failure.

Reinvigorating tired and discouraged people requires leaders to lead by example.

Fourth, Joshua demonstrates perseverance (verses 18–27)

God commanded Joshua to hold his javelin towards Ai and not to lower it until the battle had been successfully fought. Perhaps it was a pre-arranged signal, another detail in the task of necessary ongoing communication. One reason given for their success was that 'Joshua did not draw back the hand that held out his javelin until he had destroyed all who lived in Ai' (verse 26). His arm must have ached and his whole body must have been racked with tiredness. But he perseveres and doesn't give up until total victory is won.

We will only inspire others in any worthwhile way if we persevere. The leader who inspires others with a project this month, only to get excited by a different one the next, and then soon changes his or her mind and enthuses about the latest fashionable teaching or strategy doing the rounds of the conference circuit, is likely only to leave a trail of tired and disappointed people behind them. Such leaders are like the 'grand old Duke of York' who marched the troops up to the top of the hill, only to lead them down again.

In order genuinely to inspire people, perseverance is needed.

Manipulation versus inspiration

Throughout this we learn the difference between manipulation and inspiration. When leaders manipulate, they engineer people's consent for reasons that are less than transparent and often connected with a crass vision, short-term opportunism or even personal gain. Genuine inspiration does not use people, but takes them seriously. It communicates God's Word to them carefully, sets before them a mature vision, talks with them fully, identifies with them completely and works alongside them steadily until the task is complete.

Joshua truly is a model of how to revitalize a weary, discouraged people. The chapter is full of insight as it covers the issues of encouragement, obedience, adaptability, communication, sensitivity, identification, example and perseverance, and so much more. We are involved in a spiritual battle, the outcome of which is utterly secure because Christ died and then rose again. Yet the warfare continues until he returns, and part of the leader's task is to inspire the troops to persevere, even after setbacks, in the sure and certain hope of complete victory one day over the forces that are opposed to God.

Questions for reflection

1. Do I have a ministry of encouragement? If not, is it because I myself am discouraged?
2. How far am I 'one of the people' and how far do I bark orders at them from above?
3. Am I a manipulator or an authentic inspirer of others who genuinely seeks to allow people freedom in their response?

14. Renew vision (Joshua 8:30–35)

Bill Hybels, the founding pastor of Willow Creek Community Church, has devoted a great deal of energy to questions of leadership. In his book *Courageous Leadership*, he describes vision as being 'at the very core of leadership. Take vision away from a leader,' he writes, 'and you cut out his heart. Vision is the fuel that leaders run on. It's the energy that creates action.'[1] He calls the power of vision 'a leader's most potent weapon'.[2]

Reawakening vision is what the covenant renewal ceremony, which took place at Mount Ebal after victory at Ai, is all about. The details may seem remote, even boring, to us. Why Mount Ebal? Why an altar of uncut stones? Why all those offerings? What was the ark of the covenant doing there? Wasn't reading the book of the law tedious? Why were women, children and foreigners (immigrants, as we would call them today) required to be there? But every detail is a skilful exhibition in the art of casting and renewing vision. At Mount Ebal, Joshua reminded the Israelites of their distinct identity, renewed their commitment to God and recast the vision for the future.

The placing of the covenant renewal ceremony here, as Dale Ralph Davis has noted, is rather like the interruption of a TV programme with a newsflash. We're 'wrenched from conquest to covenant' and, after the ceremony, normal service is going to be resumed. But with this interruption, Israel is learning something of vital importance to its continuing prosperity. 'The writer is saying Israel's success does not primarily consist in knocking off Canaanites but in everyone's total submission to the law of God.'[3] They are being reminded of who they are and of their unique relationship with God.

Let's look at the details and pick up some clues of how to cast and renew vision.

The importance of the occasion

Two things stand out about the occasion: the where and the who.

The 'where' is Mount Ebal, which is usually identified as being near Shechem and therefore considerably north of Ai. So Joshua and the people were no longer nibbling at the edges of Canaan, but had moved deep into its territory. The location, then, symbolized the progress they had made, and communicated something more profound at the same time. It was there that Joshua 'built an altar to the LORD, the God of Israel' (verse 30), and by doing so was sending out the message that he was 'establishing the claim of the Covenant Lord over all Canaan'.[4] The God whom Israel served was not a petty tribal deity, but one who had a claim over all tribes and nations as their Creator and sovereign Judge. He would rule 'from sea to sea', and 'all kings [would] bow down to him and all nations [would] serve him'.[5] Mount Ebal was also significant because Moses had commanded Israel to build an altar there when they had crossed over into the land.[6] So this was a testimony to God's faithfulness and the fulfilment of his promise as well as the vision that Moses had had. Marking the stages reached in the fulfilment of any vision is important.

The 'who' was everybody (verse 33). The 'elders, officials and judges', together with the priests, may have had ringside seats, given their role and responsibilities in the community, but everyone was required to be present, irrespective of gender (men and women), age (parents and children) or ethnicity (native Israelites and 'foreigners living among them'). One can picture Rahab and her family among the crowd, together with many unnamed non-Israelites who had chosen to reside among them. The ceremony was of such importance that all were expected to witness it.

In casting or reawakening a vision, attention needs to be given to such practical details. The location may reinforce the vision or undermine it. The church I attend is about to build a new facility at great cost to its members. We have been inspired by visiting the empty plot of land we've bought and marking the new church out with tape, planting a cross there and praying about it. The enthusiasm levels would not have risen as much if we had remained in our old, inadequate building and merely dreamed of it. Location matters. So too does the number of people who can attend. It's no good choosing a date to cast a vision when half the people are going to be absent. They won't get the message! Energy needs to be spent on communicating the importance of everyone getting the message, just as here where Joshua ensured that 'the whole assembly of Israel' attended.

The choreography of the event

The event is choreographed with great care, with special emphasis on the way in which every detail conforms to the instructions Moses left.[7] It begins with the laying out of the stage and with preparation of an altar of 'uncut stones, on which no iron tool had been used' (verse 31). The command not to cut, dress or beautify the stones in any way is intended to prevent people from interposing themselves in worship.[8] What begins with a slight tidying up of the altar can quickly end up with the altar becoming an artistic creation and itself an object of veneration that displaces God as the sole object of worship, as with many a beautiful church building or impressive organ.

The ark of the covenant is centre stage, with the people gathering around it. Altar and ark are the focal points, to be accompanied before long by a number of stones on which the law will be written.

The altar is used for the offering of two kinds of sacrifices. The burnt offerings remind Israel that they are not their own, but belong wholly to the Lord, symbolized by the sacrificial animal being wholly consumed by fire, with nothing kept back. The fellowship offerings are more communal events, bringing the people together in celebration. So worshipping at the altar involves both a vertical (Godward) and a horizontal (peopleward) dimension.

Either while the sacrifices were being offered or just afterwards, 'Joshua wrote on stones a copy of the law of Moses' (verse 32). We know that copying out 'the basic covenant document' for all to see was a common feature of such ceremonies at the time,[9] and Israel had a good reason for following this pattern.[10] The laws would remind Israel of their essential obligations towards their covenant God, and of the terms on which they would experience his blessing, or alternatively his curse. It set out what made them distinct from other peoples. Few among them would have been literate, so necessarily, having written the law, Joshua then reads it to the people. From what is said, it probably means that he read Deuteronomy 28 – 30 to them, rather than the whole of the books of Moses.

The purpose of the whole event was to bless the people and encourage them in their further obedience to the Lord.

The significance for Joshua

We should not make too much of this, but from a leadership viewpoint it is worth remarking that while Joshua is not, and certainly never will be, a Moses, he positions himself again as being in continuity with him.[11] He is never presented as a radical departure from his mentor, but as a legitimate successor, carrying on his work and taking it to the next stage of fulfilment. Here the connection is seen not only in his teaching the people the law of Moses, but also in his own obedience to it and embodiment of it. As we might say today, he had 'bought into' the vision he was selling to others. In presiding at this ceremony, Joshua was not acting a part, however professional. He believed in what was being said and enacted. He owned the vision himself. Others will not own a vision unless those who cast it are known to be authentic.

Reflections for today

Few of us may be called to articulate a new vision, but we will be regularly called upon to reawaken a vision that has faded. We will be called to set the little work in which we are engaged within the context of the grand vision of God's salvation, of the good news of his Son, Jesus, and of his plan for the renewal of creation. When things become routine, when service becomes a chore and mission begins to drift, it is time to renew the true vision.

One of the features of this episode that we are likely to miss is the power of symbols in casting a vision. Three great physical symbols are central in this covenant renewal ceremony: the altar, the ark and the law. The altar spoke of their identity as a people who wholly belonged to the Lord, as well as their need for atonement and the blessing of communal celebration. The ark spoke of the presence of their covenant God, reigning among them from his throne, as well as the provision of God, since it contained a sample of manna with which he had fed them through the wilderness.[12] The law, both written and read, spoke of their covenant obligations as well as defining the values by which they would live and treat others. None of this was vague. Each of the symbols was tangible and stood for actual realities.

At the heart of our faith we still have the powerful symbols of baptismal water and of bread and wine. Many Christians also display the symbol of the cross in some way. But whether we can point to such symbols or not, vision casting requires the use of symbolic language. As Kouzes and Posner say, using Martin Luther King's 'I have a dream' speech as an example,

> Leaders make full use of the power of symbolic language to communicate a shared identity, and give life to visions. They use metaphors, tell stories and relate anecdotes; they draw word pictures; and they offer quotations and recite slogans. They enable constituents to picture the future, to hear it, to sense it, to recognize it.[13]

To cast a vision is 'to paint a compelling picture of the future, one that enables constituents to experience . . . what it would be like to actually live and work in an exciting and uplifting future'.[14] And to do that, we need to set in front of people not only a picture of the future, but also, according to Ken

Blanchard, a significant purpose and a set of clear values.[15] That's exactly what the altar, the ark and the law do for Israel.

If Joshua reflected in some measure the leadership of Moses, most of us will only ever be a pale reflection of the leadership of Joshua. But it's worth learning from him how to revitalize a vision that may have grown stale – a vision not just of the immediate future of our local church or favoured organization, since, ultimately, they are bound to pass away, but a vision of a renewed creation when God has banished all evil and we live eternally in the new heavens and the new earth.

Now that's a real vision to inspire, a great vision worth working for.

Questions for reflection

1. What is the vision I cast for the people I lead?
2. Do people own the vision for themselves or do I have to remind them of it endlessly? If so, is there a way to encourage them to own it for themselves?
3. Could I make better use of symbols and ceremonies in recasting vision?

15. Correct mistakes (Joshua 9:1–27)

It is an encouragement to me when I see that great leaders make mistakes. I know that I've a long way to go before I am perfectly sanctified! I don't mean that I rejoice in their faults and failures, but I'm encouraged because these serve as a reminder that not even the greatest of leaders will get it right all the time. I'm certainly no exception. Nor was Joshua.

All leaders, apart from Christ, are fallible, a fact that should liberate us from the cosh of perfectionism. Perfectionists are sometimes so paralysed with fear that they may do something wrong, that they are afraid to do anything at all. The resulting inaction often makes a situation that could have been relatively easily handled worse, or leaves other people confused and uncertain. Then, sometimes, when perfectionists do make decisions and take action and they go wrong, they beat themselves up and can slide into depression. Perfectionists don't make good leaders. So while we should aim for the highest of standards, we should also be realistic in our expectations and accept that, however diligent we are, we will not be unerringly right all the time.

Joshua's failure occurred when he was visited by a delegation of Gibeonites who sought a treaty with Israel. With hindsight, this failure may have been glaring, but the valuable thing for us is that he not only fails, but gives some pointers as to how a failure can be rescued. Let's look at what we can learn from the incident.

The failure of Joshua's leadership

It's often easy enough after the event to identify where things have gone wrong, although good leadership should anticipate the pitfalls and potential problems and seek to avoid them if at all possible. The Gibeonites were near neighbours belonging to the Hivite people, who lived in a city about six miles northwest of Jerusalem, but pretended to live much further away. And thereby hangs the tale. They came to Joshua with what appeared to be a sensible and honest request for an alliance, and to all appearances – they had ensured the make-up and props departments made them fit the part they wanted to play – they had travelled far, and their explanation for the request was plausible. So Joshua made a treaty with them (verse 15). No sooner had he done so, just three days later in fact, than their story began to unravel, and Joshua, having been duped, was left red-faced. Why did the mistake occur?

Three failures conspired to lead to the mistake.

First, there was a failure to consult the Lord

Verse 14 is quite explicit about this: 'The Israelites . . . did not enquire of the Lord.' They relied on their own wisdom and went ahead in making their decision without stopping to pray about it. The instructions they had received from the Lord had made it abundantly clear that there was to be no compromise with the current occupants of the land. That alone should have given them a reason to pause. But they rushed ahead without taking God or his word into account. What happened as a result was that the Gibeonites were allowed to set the agenda rather than following the one set by the Lord himself, and a small colony from a neighbouring pagan nation were welcomed to live right at the heart of their community, like the proverbial Trojan Horse.

Their second failure was a failure to investigate the facts

When the Gibeonites came to them dressed in worn-out clothes, carrying dry, cracked wineskins and munching food that was well past its sell-by date, everything seemed to suggest they had travelled a great distance. In fairness, Joshua did probe a little and ask them for some confirmation of their story, only to be rewarded with outright lies. The failure seems to have been that the Israelites did not probe deeply enough and were sucked in too easily. Joshua and his colleagues were somewhat gullible.

When I look back on my ministry as both a pastor and a leader of organizations, I can readily see how easily mistakes were made when we made assumptions and did not enquire deeply enough, instead taking people's words at face value. Pastorally, we can often miss connections between people, or assume hidden histories that lead to pastoral nightmares because we did not ask realistic questions. We sometimes discover the complexity of relationships, or the backlog of resentments, too late when another pastoral crisis occurs or we're on the verge of taking a delicate wedding or funeral. It pays to ask and not presume. In leadership terms, we can make presumptions that cost us dearly because we have not probed vested interests, have been presented 'innocently' with only one solution rather than options, have not done due diligence on an appointment, or have taken someone's word that something has been done without asking for the evidence. Present-day business and public service put a high premium on 'due diligence', and with good reason. And so should we. Leaders should be very wary about making assumptions.

The third element of Joshua's failure was, in fact, a failure to use common sense

The commentator Marten Woudstra points this out. As mentioned above, the story hinges on the distance the Gibeonites had travelled and, as Woudstra remarks, 'Joshua was probably naïve in not perceiving that the Gibeonites, if from such a distance as they claimed, were not actually in need of a treaty.'[1] He's right. Common sense seems to have deserted Joshua at this moment: if they had really travelled as far as they had claimed, Israel would not have had them in her sights and no treaty would have been needed. A treaty was only needed if they were nearby occupants of the land, and that would have raised an entirely different set of issues. If only Joshua and his colleagues had used their heads!

Sometimes leaders take foolish decisions because they allow their hearts to rule their heads. They act with good intent and out of spiritual zeal, but forget that God is not only the God of the supernatural and remarkable, but the God who has given us minds, renewed by the Spirit, to think things through. His down-to-earth wisdom is part of inspired Scripture. The book of Proverbs encourages careful thought and intelligent planning as we reach decisions and look to the future.[2] We do not honour God by failing to use our intelligence.

David Firth somewhat damningly says that this 'is a textbook example of how the people of God should *not* make decisions'.[3] Granting that, the story also provides a textbook example of how to redeem your mistakes, as far as you can.

The wisdom of Joshua's leadership

The first step on the road to recovery

Wisely, Joshua listened to his people (verses 16–19) and took note of their grumbling. Suspicions remained and rumours abounded about these visitors from a distance. The ordinary people seemed to know what their leaders didn't, which was that they weren't who they said they were and in fact came from just down the road, as it were. The people of Israel set out to investigate and found the Hivite cities from which they came pretty quickly. Mercifully, the people restrained their anger and didn't attack those cities, remembering the commitment to peace that Joshua had made.

There are times when it is right to take the risk and refuse to reopen a discussion that was well rehearsed when the decision was taken. Some committees delight in doing nothing better than revisiting previous decisions and unmaking them endlessly, thereby achieving nothing except to encourage inertia and cause confusion. But there are times when it is right to listen to the unease of the people we are leading and not press ahead, especially if, as here, there is compelling fresh evidence which makes the case for a reconsideration of a decision obvious. Leaders can live in a bubble. They can see only what their advisors put in front of them and hear only voices that the gatekeepers have let through. Ordinary people often have a good deal more nous about situations than leaders, and wise leaders never isolate themselves from the people they lead.

The second step on the road to recovery

When confronted with his people's findings, what was Joshua to do? He faced a dilemma. However precipitously, he had given his word to the Gibeonites and would not break his promise, or his word would be worth nothing (verse 19) and his leadership would lack integrity. He takes the second step on the road to recovery by showing the need to live with his mistake while mitigating it as much as he could. It is probably true, as Davis claims, that people in Joshua's day had a higher view of giving their word than we do in the contemporary Western world.[4] If so, more's the pity.

Whatever our culture finds acceptable, however, as Christian leaders we need to be people of integrity who keep our word. Using Jesus as his benchmark,[5] Paul explained to the Corinthians that he did not make his plans 'in a worldly manner' and change them as he thought fit, but was faithful to what he had promised with his 'yes' meaning 'yes' and his 'no' meaning 'no'.[6] So only in the most compelling of circumstances should we go back on our promises. Those circumstances may include when we are made aware that we have taken a decision on a very faulty, indeed sinful, basis, or when new evidence comes to light that makes complete nonsense of the previous decision. Jephthah's vow, which resulted in the death of his daughter, is interesting in this respect.[7]

The third step on the road to recovery

His integrity intact, Joshua then summoned the Gibeonites and confronted the issue (verses 22–27). He did not, as many leaders try to do, sweep it under the carpet. His righteous anger is made perfectly clear to them, and he places them under a curse. They respect his right to do so and throw themselves on his mercy. His judgment was that they would continue to enjoy the peace he had promised, but that they would not do so as a free people but as menial servants of the Israelites. His wise decision means he is able successfully to negotiate the precipice and avoid falling off, either on one side into excessive leniency by breaking his word, or on the other into excessive severity by condemning them to death. His judgment is mixed with mercy, and his righteous mercy is free from sentimentality.

Reflecting on his successful negotiation of the Northern Ireland Agreement, which brought years of conflict to an end, Tony Blair writes, 'At the heart of any conflict resolution must be a framework based on agreed principles. One of the things I always try to do in politics is to get back to first principles: what is it really about? What are we trying to achieve? What is at the heart of the matter?'[8] He adds, 'In conflict resolution, small things can be big things. This is not just about gripping, it is also about putting aside your view of what is important in favour of theirs. And not being prissy about finding such things below your pay grade. Your pay grade covers anything important to the parties you are serving; as defined by them.'[9]

Joshua acts just as Tony Blair was later to advise. He acts on the principles of integrity and righteousness. He shows concern for the issues that have stirred up his people, whether they were justified in their reaction or not. He does not reward sin, and yet shows mercy. He works with the mistake made, but brings as much good out of the situation as possible.

A clue to Joshua's success

Why did Joshua navigate his way out of the mistake so easily and not get bogged down in it? For one thing, it is evident that he had built up a huge fund of goodwill, and the people, both the Israelites and the Gibeonites, trusted him and his judgment. That's important. Some leaders undermine the trust of the people they are leading by a succession of bad judgments and mistakes. It is as if they are constantly depleting the bank account, where the capital consists of trust, not money, and never replenishing it. When this happens, a leader doesn't have to make a huge withdrawal before finding that he or she is into an overdraft situation. That's why people can sometimes appear very patient with leaders when they make big mistakes, but then become impatient over a trivial mistake. The trust fund is empty. We must take care to build our leadership capital by investing in gaining our people's trust, so that when a mistake or failure happens, we don't end up with nothing left in the bank of goodwill, but find, as Joshua did, that we are still supported and able to enjoy the people's confidence.

The value of failure

The truth is that not only is no leader infallible, but failures can be turned into positive learning experiences. As Kouzes and Posner point out, whether it be sports, games, education or work,

> People never do anything perfectly the first time they try it . . .
>
> Over and again, people in our studies tell us how important mistakes and failure have been to their success. Without mistakes we'd be unable to know what we can and what we cannot do . . . without those experiences, respondents said, they would never have been able to achieve their aspirations. It may seem ironic but many echo the thought that the overall quality of work improves when people have a chance to fail . . . 'It is failure which breeds success.'
>
> We don't advocate for a moment that failure ought to be the objective of any endeavour. The objective is *learning*.[10]

We should never set out to fail. But if we do, we can learn from our mistakes and put into practice the sort of response we find modelled by Joshua. Above all, let's ensure that we have such a good relationship with the people we lead, and that we have built the fund of trust, so that if mistakes are made, people will forgive us and move forwards with us, under our continuing leadership, into a new, more positive day.

Questions for reflection

1. Am I a perfectionist or am I able to cope with my limitations and recognize that I will make mistakes?
2. Can I distinguish between times when I need to revisit a decision and admit I got it wrong and times when I need to stick to it?
3. When I have made an error, how do I seek to repair it? Do I try to ignore or deny it?
4. Do past failures hold me back from serving Christ confidently today?

16. Fight battles (Joshua 10:1 – 12:24)

There are some outstanding individuals who have the ability to apply their leadership skills across a range of areas, and move effortlessly from success in business, to the arts, to education, to manufacturing or whatever. Leadership consists of a skill set that is transferable to several different fields. Most of us, however, tend to be effective leaders in only one field because we combine practised leadership skills with an acute understanding of the culture of that field. Every area has its own way of doing things, its own language, its own way of perceiving the world, its own customs and rituals. To be effective, a leader has to enter into that culture, even if, once they have earned people's trust, they want to change it. The failure to enter a culture explains why some very gifted leaders are not successful when they change from one sphere of work to another, or even from one local church to another. They never make the necessary adjustment.[1]

Joshua excels as a military leader. His skills are not restricted to the battlefield since, as we shall see, he ably exploits the administrative gift that is inherent in being a military tactician.

Nonetheless, it is as a military commander that he excels, as a major central section of the book of Joshua records.

The range of Joshua's battles

Joshua's victories are listed in some detail. In brief, they are:

- defeat of the Amorite alliance (10:1–27)
- conquest of the southern cities (10:28–43)
- capture of the northern territories (11:1–23)
- victories in the east of Jordan reviewed (12:1–6)
- victories in the west of Jordan reviewed (12:7–24).

While there remained a little land to be conquered,[2] virtually the 'entire land' had been taken and it was fair to say that 'the land had rest from war' (11:23).

The key to Joshua's success

We will never be called upon to become literal soldiers, fighting for the Lord, as Joshua was. Even so, we will be called upon to fight battles of a different kind within our organizations and groups, on administrative, practical, relational and visionary fronts. More particularly, we are called to engage in the spiritual battles that are not of the 'flesh-and-blood' variety, which Paul describes in Ephesians 6:10–18. If we want a life of ease, we should never become leaders. Leaders are fighters. This should never be because they are aggressive or angular characters, but because leadership inevitably has to fight against opposing forces. If we meet no other foe, we shall meet the forces of inertia. But we're also likely to meet more stubborn resistance to any plans that suggest we move God's people forwards, opposition that arises from human, worldly and satanic sources. While it is true that we remain in a constant state of war, the intensity of the fighting may vary, as it does in any war. But we always need to be on our guard, so that when the enemy attacks, we are ready to respond.

In the light of this, we would do well to pay attention to the reasons for Joshua's success. We could discuss the way in which he does not fight on all fronts at once, but engages in a series of discrete campaigns, targeting particular regions one after the other. We could discuss the way he picks his battles or follows through on his victories, as illustrated in 10:22–27, for example. We could mention the element of surprise that he used, as illustrated by 11:7. We could comment on his perseverance, since 11:18 mentions that 'Joshua waged war against all these kings *for a long time*' (italics mine). He did not give up easily. These are at least hinted at as elements that were key to his success, even if they are not explicitly stated, in the report of his campaigns. But much of this would be reading into the text, the interest of which seems to lie elsewhere. The truth is that it lists his victories, but tells us virtually nothing about his military strategies or tactics. The focus is on the spiritual keys to his success, and this makes it much more immediately applicable to the type of leadership in which we will engage.

These chapters make the Lord the centre of attention, and the relationship between Joshua and his Lord, who is the real commander of the armies of Israel,[3] proves crucial. In fact, the Lord is mentioned nineteen times.

Four features are emphasized.

Joshua obeys the Lord

In view of what we've been learning of Joshua's leadership journey up to now, this is unsurprising. Obedience may justifiably be claimed to be the running theme of these reports. It is explicitly referred to in 10:19, 25, 40; 11:6, 9, 12, 15 and 23. The focus is sometimes on his obeying the immediate command of God about a particular battle, for example, in 11:9, but this is in the context of a wider stance of obedience to all that Moses had enshrined in his laws and prophecies. Dale Ralph Davis puts his finger on this when, agreeing with Trent Butler,[4] he comments on 11:15:

> That seems to be what verse 15 is saying: 'Here is a model of God's servant. His chief characteristic is that he obeys God's commands.' That sounds bland and nonthreatening enough, and common place. But it stands as a needed witness to Israel's future leaders and kings . . . that what marks a model leader is not the size of his chariot forces, the number of females in his harem, or the presence of peacocks in the royal zoo, but an obedience to God's commandments that leads God's people to be faithful.[5]

If this was a needed lesson for Israel's leaders, it remains a needed lesson for contemporary leadership too. The trappings and baubles of leadership so often assume more importance than obedience, either in the eyes of the people being led or in the eyes of the leader him- or herself. Joshua is exemplary because of his strict obedience.

Joshua waits for the Lord

As an experienced general, Joshua might have been expected to make the decisions about when to attack and the particular tactics to be adopted. But 11:6–7 shows us the way in which, in spite of that, Joshua still waits for the Lord's instructions about particular battles and the tactics to be adopted, which can vary from battle to battle. He does not rely on his own understanding. Once the instruction has been received, we see Joshua obeying it without delay. Once again we read the formula: 'The LORD said to Joshua . . . So Joshua' did what the Lord commanded.

Joshua enjoys victory from the Lord

The record of his military conquests moves easily back and forth between recognizing the part Joshua played and the part God himself played in granting them victory. Joshua's contribution is not airbrushed out of the account, and we often read words like: 'So Joshua subdued the whole region' (10:40); 'At that time, Joshua turned back and captured Hazor' (11:10); 'So Joshua took the entire land' (11:16, 23); 'Joshua waged war against all these kings . . .' (11:18); and 'Here is a list of the kings of the land that Joshua and the Israelites conquered' (12:7). David Howard remarks, 'The emphasis on Joshua is striking.'[6] Indeed it is. Joshua is highlighted as the human agent through whom God brings about the victory.

This contrasts with some forms of super-spiritual Christianity that ignore the servants of God and their contribution, and consider them not worthy of acknowledgment. It was summed up in that prayer which an old deacon supposedly prayed before a service, 'Thank you, Lord, for sending your servant Mike Jones to preach this morning, but now blot him out, that we may see Jesus only.' If I've not heard those exact words, I've heard something very like them more than once! It leaves you wondering why you needed to go at all if that was what they wanted. A truer biblical understanding is that God uses people, and they should be treated with respect and honour, and it is right to recognize their contribution.

Having said that, in the balance between the human and divine elements in ensuring victory here, there is no doubt that the scales weigh in favour of the Lord. It is he who ultimately grants the victories to Israel, and he who gives them rest in the land he has promised them. It is his word on which they rely as they go into battle and which gives them the assurance of victory: 'I have given them into your hand. Not one of them will be able to withstand you' (10:8); 'Do not be afraid of them [the northern kings], because by this time tomorrow I will hand all of them, slain, over to Israel' (11:6). Joshua's part is not to be underestimated, but the Lord's part is the determinative factor.

Joshua obtained the Lord's promise

That is the import of the concluding verse, 11:23, in this section of Joshua, before the appendix of chapter 12 is added.[7] 'So Joshua took the entire land . . . Then the land had rest from war.' The conquest of the land has permitted Joshua and all the people to inherit the land God had promised to Moses, to occupy it and enjoy a peaceful existence in it. The promise has been realized, and the hope has become a reality. They could now enter into the tangible blessings of God in a way previous generations could only have dreamed of.

Conclusion

Much could be said about the battles that leaders face and the way they should approach them. But since we are seeking to learn from Joshua and the battles he fought, one thing stands out above all else. Leaders need to fight battles in a way that is consistent with God's laws. That will lead us to reject many methods and tactics that would commonly be accepted elsewhere but are unacceptable among God's people, such as being underhand, getting even, lying or using force. Paul illustrates this principle when he claims, 'We do not use deception, nor do we distort the word of God. On the contrary, by setting forth the truth plainly we commend ourselves to everyone in the sight of God.'[8] In saying this, he was explicitly distancing himself from the tactics of some of the great orators and the teaching of the rhetorical schools of his day, and implicitly teaching that we should not adopt methods that may be common elsewhere, but rather ensure the total compatibility between our message of grace and truth, and our methods of love and integrity.

Not only are we to engage in our battles in a way that is in total alignment with the Bible's teaching about how we should behave as godly people, but we should also listen carefully to the voice of God about particular situations. We should ask, is this a battle in which we should engage or one we can leave safely in his hands, as Jehoshaphat was reminded to do?[9] We should pick our battles with care, and only when God's honour, rather than our own ego, is at stake. If we are to join forces in battle, when and how should we engage the opposition? What has the Lord to say about that? And do we enter the fray relying on our own strength and expertise, or do we know that it is the Lord alone who determines the outcome, so we trust fully in him?

I hope your battles are few. But if you have to fight, don't put on Saul's armour. Let Joshua be your model.

Questions for reflection

1. Am I prepared to get up and fight for Christ or do I, in reality, prefer to be a comfortable, armchair Christian?
2. What kinds of battles am I called to fight for Christ?
3. When engaging in spiritual warfare, do I have the right balance between divine empowerment and my human responsibility?

17. Demonstrate perseverance (Joshua 13:1–33)

Well, God certainly doesn't mince his words, does he? After all Joshua's victories, God says to him, 'You are now very old . . .' (verse 1)! I can imagine Joshua replying, 'Thanks, God, for the reminder. Actually my battle-worn body tells me that every day.' God does not say this to discourage Joshua, but rather to inspire him to persevere and to see that he still has work to do.

We do not know how old Joshua was when God spoke to him. But age is obviously a significant issue, since the word 'old' is used twice in verse 1. He was probably similar in age to Caleb, whom we know to be eighty-five around this time.[1] We know that Joshua died at the age of 110.[2] So he has another potential twenty-five years of life and leadership left in him. And that's the point. He's not on the scrap heap yet. He is still a leader.

God's challenge to Joshua

Whatever Joshua was expecting, God immediately makes it clear that the reference to his age is not a preamble to telling him he can hang up his boots and put on his slippers. So if he thought God had spoken to announce his retirement, he was to be disappointed, although I suspect that retirement would not have suited Joshua. God spoke to his elderly leader first to renew an old commission and second to give him a new challenge.

Joshua faces an unfinished task (verses 2–5)

There was still land that remained to be conquered on the edges of the territory they had subdued. The details may be a little unclear to us, but the point is abundantly clear. The western coastal area of the Philistines had not yet been captured. To the south there was the land of Geshur and territory which would reach down to the Egyptian border. Way up north the lands around Sidon, the country of Lebanon and the city of Byblos were yet to be brought under Israelite control.

The task was not yet complete, and so the commission God gave to Joshua still stands. A huge amount had been accomplished, but not everything. Most leaders can identify with Joshua, for however much they have achieved, unlike their Master, they can never say, 'It is finished.' That victory cry belongs to Jesus alone.[3] The fact, though, that there is always more that could be done should not stop us from being thankful for what has been achieved in Christ's name.

David Firth poses an interesting question about this. True, elements of the task remain to be fulfilled, but by emphasizing Joshua's age, was God in fact recognizing that he is no longer physically fit enough to do it? Is he reminding Joshua that he remains responsible for the job that isn't yet finished, but that he should delegate the execution of the task to others? Indeed, verse 6 states that God will drive out some of these northern inhabitants himself. The brevity of the text means we cannot be sure, but it is an interesting take on it, and this interpretation is supported by the second part of God's conversation with Joshua. If Firth is right, he is also right to contrast Joshua with Moses and Caleb, who were fighting fit right to the end. Firth insightfully comments that in Scripture, 'there is no universal pattern for understanding the relationship between age and effective ministry'.[4] We're foolish to impose one pattern on all.

Faithfulness to God does not necessarily mean that we will continue to do the same ministry in the same active way until we die. It may well mean a fresh calling from God to a form of ministry that is more appropriate to our age and increasing limitations. We must aim for resilience, a word we'll return to shortly, but that does not mean rigidity and inflexibility.

Joshua faces a new challenge (verses 6–7)

God then told Joshua that from now on he was to concern himself with the allocation of the land to the Israelites and dividing the inheritance among the nine-and-a-half tribes.[5] In this next phase Joshua is given more of a desk job. Whether that is due to his age or not, it is a recognition that the needs have changed. True, there is still some land to be conquered, but most of the land God had promised them was now in Israelite hands, so the need was to parcel it out wisely among the tribes so that they could settle in it and put down roots. The point was never about conquering the territory just to prove they could, and then leaving it empty to be turned back into a wasteland. The point was to occupy it wisely. For that to happen, some organization needed to be applied so that the various tribes didn't undo their victories by squabbling over who was going to live where. The respect in which Joshua was held, and his proven track record as a leader, made him just the right person to lead phase two of the occupation as he had successfully led phase one.

Even as an elderly leader, Joshua is still the Lord's servant. Retirement is not an option, but change is. Until his dying day, there was work to be done.

Joshua's challenge to us

Joshua challenges us to be leaders who will last the race and not give up before the end. Like him, we need to persevere and develop staying power, since, as Gordon MacDonald points out, 'It makes little difference how fast you can run the 100 metres when the race is 400 metres long. Life is not a sprint; it is a distance run', to which he adds, 'and it demands the kinds of conditioning that enables people to go the distance.'[6]

Let's understand what that means. It doesn't mean, as we have said and as Joshua demonstrates, that we'll keep doing the same thing, the same way, year in and year out until we die. Persevering means growing in God and being faithful to him as we face today's challenges and situations, not a dogged, unthinking and false loyalty to a ministry, an organization, a programme or a pattern, which was right for us yesterday but is no longer suitable. Some preachers go on preaching long past their ability to do so, and they sadly undo much of the good work they did previously. Their preaching is serving their own needs rather than the needs of the church. How much better it would be if they used their experience in different ways, perhaps in mentoring the next generation. Equally, there are people who hang on to a leadership position long after they have served God's purpose for them and when their influence has long since waned. Change can be challenging for people at any age, but it is especially challenging when we're older. Good leadership demands adaptability and responsive flexibility rather than dogged entrenchment. Still others strive to be in leadership but, once they get there, fail to exploit its potential, not changing with the needs of the time. They are like Israel would have been if they had conquered the land but not occupied it. We need to utilize the leadership we have been given by God and develop it over time.

But how? Leadership involves a constant giving out to others and, like a reservoir, it is easy to become drained unless constantly replenished by a fresh inflow of resources. Failure to keep replenished sometimes becomes apparent to others more quickly than it does to the leader him- or herself. Leaders have often developed a professionalism which has many positive advantages, but negatively means we can go through the motions long after our heart is no longer in our work. The emptiness may disguise a failing leadership, but it will not ultimately be able to prevent it from failing. Unless addressed, it will bring a person's leadership to an end. So keep refreshed, through prayer, spiritual companionship, studying God's Word, reading widely (not just for sermons) and becoming a whole person.

Bill Hybels' advice on staying the course

When Bill Hybels asked a group of senior and effective pastors what their most pressing question was, he received the surprising answer that it was about 'enduring'.[7] How could they keep going? How could they sustain their ministries, especially in view of the rapidly changing world in which they lived? Speaking out of his own experiences, he offered a four-level course in the graduate school of endurance:

- Level 1: Make your calling sure and stay focused.
- Level 2: Develop the courage to change, changing the pace of your ministry, how you do ministry, and making personal changes to your inner world and emotions.

- Level 3: Endure by discovering safe people and gather them around you.
- Level 4: Endure by adopting an eternal perspective.[8]

He concluded with the plea: 'Stay the course. Stay the course. Stay the course. If I do, – if all of us leaders do – we will win the day for the glory of the one whose name we bear.'[9]

Gordon MacDonald's wisdom on resilience

Another experienced and honed leader with a passion for this issue and the wisdom to match it is Gordon MacDonald, who urges all believers, not just leaders, to develop a resilient life. In a book packed full of spiritual insight, MacDonald exploits his athletic background to explain how we need to develop stamina in the spiritual race. Much of his advice overlaps with that of Bill Hybels, but it is fuller, since he's writing a whole book on the subject. Among other things – and this is very selective – he advises that to stay the course we need to have a sense of life-direction, to cultivate Christian character, to listen to our call from God and be confident in our gifts and generous with our lives. We need to repair the past, not live in it, and be quick to repent, forgive and be thankful, so that no unhelpful legacy hinders us in the present. MacDonald discusses the need for us to keep fit in body, mind and also in our emotions, and especially to keep 'trimming' our egos and be open to the presence of God. Like Hybels, he devotes some considerable space to the importance of cultivating friendship and valuing intimacy.

Much of what he writes is like pearls strung out on the connecting thread of self-discipline. His conclusion consists of a letter he composed to his old college athletic coach, albeit years after the coach had died. In it he wrote, 'And thanks for the constant emphasis on self-discipline and for making it clear that if I would push myself, I would not only be an athlete, but a person God could use as He filled me with his Spirit.'[10]

'Resilient people are committed to finishing strong.'[11] But that doesn't just happen. It happens when we develop stamina, practise intentionality, train daily, never let up on obedience and cultivate godliness.

As Gordon MacDonald says, 'Quitting is not an option. "Walking" is unthinkable.'[12] I rather think that Joshua would agree.

Questions for reflection

1. Am I a sprinter or a marathon runner?
2. Do I start but never finish things? Do I give up too easily? If so, why?
3. Am I able to adapt to new challenges, appropriate to new callings and stages in life?
4. What factors am I building into my life to ensure 'resilience'?

18. Manage administration
(Joshua 13:8 – 19:51)

I was best man to a friend who, I am convinced, was born as an administrator. In my toast I pictured him proposing to his fiancée, clipboard in hand, spreadsheet at the ready, pen behind the ear, and box to tick as to whether she said yes or no, with routes through a lengthy questionnaire depending on her answer. The guests clearly enjoyed the picture because they knew it was true to him! There may be few of us who like administration. Most of us would prefer to be on the front line. Many of us find administration boring and, at best, a necessary chore. So we're grateful for those who have the gift to manage administration on our behalf.

Administration is a gift from God

Joshua would almost certainly have preferred to be on the front line, since he was, after all, supremely a soldier. But having conquered virtually all the territory God had promised Israel (see previous chapter), God now instructs him to become an administrator. Armies, of course, depend on administrators to work out the logistics, provide the supplies, arrange the transport and ensure good communications. Without them, any army is bound to fail, as some notable battles in history demonstrate. And when the battle is won, administrators become even more important. The Iraq War provides ample evidence of that. Winning the war in Iraq was one thing, but reconstructing the country afterwards and rebuilding its physical and political infrastructure was something completely different. The Western allies may have been successful in the first, but were lamentably unprepared for the second, and so failed ultimately to achieve their objectives.

Here we have reached a significantly new stage in Joshua's career. His new job description made him responsible for the administrative management of allocating the land and dividing it up among the tribes (13:6–7). We need to recognize that this is as much the call of God on his life as destroying Jericho, conquering Ai and capturing enemy kings. The text is explicit. God tells him to do this, 'as I have instructed you'. Some of us need to realize that administration is as much a gift and a calling from God as is fighting on the front line.[1]

If Joshua had not obeyed this instruction, the conquest of Canaan would have been a futile waste of effort and without purpose. Why fight and take possession unless you are going to occupy the land, live in it, make your home there and cultivate it so that it provides food for you and your families?

Joshua as an example of good administration

Settling the land required administrative skills. And while these chapters are not written as a management textbook, they do provide some interesting insights into the skills

required by Christian leaders who have to manage administration. Let me highlight seven features that characterize
Joshua's administration.

Joshua has a comprehensive vision of the problem

He sets about his task in a systematic way, keeping everything
relevant within his sights. He does not miss anything that is
likely to trip him up later and does not neglect anyone. He
deals with the settlement tribe by tribe, providing each with
clear boundaries so they can see their place in relation
to others. One of the qualities that exceptional footballers
possess is good peripheral vision. Leaders also need that skill,
so that while focusing on particular tasks they are not unaware
of the broad picture, which could, if ignored, cause their
decisions to unravel.

Joshua reaches his decisions impartially

In parcelling out the land, he shows no favouritism towards
his own tribe or to any of the others, but acts with integrity,
ensuring a just settlement for all. His handling of the last
phase of the settlement process seems to stress this, but is
probably illustrative of his administration throughout. The
seven tribes who were the last to settle were given an equitable
distribution of the land (18:3–6). Conversely, the Levites were
given no land (18:7), in accordance with God's detailed and
meticulous commands,[2] even though, I suspect, Joshua might
have been subject to pressure from them to bend the rules.

Leaders must be even-handed at all times. So we need to
be very cautious when we face a conflict of interests in making
decisions, perhaps because a family member or a pet project
is involved. Just as God is impartial in his judgments,[3] so
his representatives need to be impartial in their decisions.
James describes wisdom that comes from heaven not only as

'peace-loving, considerate, submissive, full of mercy and good fruit', but also as 'impartial and sincere'.[4] We need to be very suspicious of our biases and perhaps step aside from taking some decisions where people might suspect us, rightly or wrongly, of being motivated by personal advantage.

Joshua keeps earlier promises

The report makes a point of highlighting this. It is neither taken for granted nor insignificant. In the first half of the account, the allocation of the land is repeatedly prefaced by a phrase like: 'This is what Moses had given to the tribe of . . .',[5] while Caleb's story draws attention to Joshua fulfilling the promise Moses made to him (14:9–13). If the reference to Moses is largely omitted in the rest of the report, the use of the words 'allotted' and 'inheritance' continues to emphasize that what Joshua was doing was keeping the earlier promises made by Moses.

As Henry and Richard Blackaby comment, 'A sure way for a leader to forfeit his influence is to make careless promises . . . Followers soon recognize such people and disregard everything they say.'[6] Such promises are both easily made and easily broken. But their effect is to lead to cynicism and disillusion. Wise administrators are careful about the promises they make, and even more careful about keeping them. Do not claim what cannot be delivered.

Joshua allocates scarce resources according to need

The allocation appears to have proceeded smoothly until Joshua receives a complaint from the tribe of Joseph. Leaders will always encounter discontented moaners at some stage. The people of Joseph insist that they need a larger allocation of land (17:14–18). They do not make their case by appealing to any promise made by the Lord or by Moses or by citing any precedent, but purely on their own 'subjective evaluation' that their numbers require it.[7] But Joshua holds the line and continues to allocate the land impartially, in accordance with promises made. All administrators know how uncomfortable challenges from pressure groups can be, especially when the complainants confront them in person, and strongly, even passionately, argue for a decision to be changed. Consequently, administrators need to have the confidence that they are on sure ground when challenged in this way.

Joshua avoids creating dependency

When the complaining people of Joseph didn't let up, Joshua told them the solution lay within their own hands (17:16–18). In fact, he turns the tables and uses their complaint against them. If they are so numerous, he says, they have the labour they need to clear the forested hill country and occupy that. They also have the fighting force they'd need to free it from the Canaanites, even though the Canaanites might have the military advantage due to their technology. Joshua does not take steps to do what they should rightly do for themselves. Being overly helpful can prevent people from growing to maturity and keep them as children who expect others to do everything for them. Good administration avoids this trap.

There are other places in these chapters which hint at this being Joshua's regular stance. In 16:10, when Ephraim failed to dislodge the Canaanites from their territory, Joshua does not step in to help them, although undoubtedly he could have done so. They need to take responsibility for themselves.

Good administration does not remove responsibility from people, but is used to enable them to grow in the acceptance of their own responsibility.

Joshua takes initiatives and incites others to action

The land distribution seems to have started well, but the beginning of chapter 18 suggests that progress stalled. Israel had encamped at Shiloh, and it seems that seven tribes 'who had not yet received their inheritance' were reluctant to move away from there and take possession of what was theirs. Joshua challenges them with the words: 'How long will you wait before you begin to take possession of the land that the LORD, the God of your ancestors, has given you?' (verse 3). It sounds like an accusation.[8] Why were they holding back? Was it laziness, lack of courage,[9] or perhaps just a sense of being comfortable where they were?

Whatever the explanation, Joshua finds it unacceptable that God has made such a provision for them and they are not making any effort to avail themselves of it. This was no way to treat God! But he does more than stir them up; he takes steps to overcome their lethargy and inaction. Three people are appointed from each of the tribes and are given the responsibility of surveying the land and then returning to Joshua with an accurate description of it so that it can be divided up between them. That's a point worth noting. Good leaders not only challenge their people to greater achievements, but also take practical steps to enable them to accomplish those achievements. Too many preachers challenge their congregations frequently, but neither suggest positive steps they can take to rectify the condition they condemn so vigorously, nor lift a finger to offer practical help.

Joshua shows dependence on God throughout his allocation of the land

Joshua took all his decisions, conscious of the presence of God and the need to obey God's revealed will. But as the report of the settlement comes to a conclusion, one practice character-izes it. When the remaining land is divided into seven parts, the actual allocation among the tribes is determined by the casting of lots. While this may seem to us a strange and un-necessary procedure, its value was that God alone would determine the outcome of the lot. They did not see it in any way as related to chance, but rather as an exercise in God's sovereignty. Proverbs 16:33 neatly expresses their under-standing of what happens when lots are cast: 'The lot is cast into the lap, but its every decision is from the LORD.'

We no longer need to rely on lots as a way of determining God's verdict on our questions, since we have the benefit of the Holy Spirit dwelling within us, both individually and corporately as the body of Christ, to guide us. Nonetheless, the same principle of total dependence on, and obedience to, God continues to apply to all leaders.

Leadership and management

Never despise the importance of good administration, since it can make or mar any progress, any advance and any victory a leader accomplishes. Leaders are usually, like Joshua, essentially pioneers, and so are not always good managers or administrators. Some may even be impatient with adminis-tration, since it seems to slow things down, divert energies and address detailed questions that big-picture leaders don't see as significant. It is quite common in contemporary leader-ship training to contrast leaders and managers along the following lines:

Leaders	*Managers*
Practise an art	Practise a science
Provide vision	Provide realism

Leaders	Managers
Provide direction	Provide control
Deal in ideas	Deal in functions
Exercise faith	Work with facts
Seek effectiveness	Seek efficiency
Find opportunities and resources	Use available resources

There is value in this clear categorization, although I am not wholly convinced by the analysis. In reality, the boundary line between the two is much more blurred, and most of us work in much smaller-scale operations where we are required to be both leaders and managers, In such a situation, neglecting one side at the expense of the other is to our organization's detriment. However, it is worth saying that if you are a visionary leader and do not have the gift of management and administration yourself, make sure you find people to work with you who have. Don't be irritated by them, since they will approach things very differently from you, but welcome them as colleagues whose contribution not only complements yours but strengthens your success. The same is equally true in the reverse direction. If your default stance is that of an administrator, you will need to be complemented by a visionary leader, or you may maintain and preserve what you inherit but never advance it. Managers may find visionary leaders frustrating and naive. But the combination offers great strength.[10]

The qualities of good administrative leaders today

This is a suitable point at which to summarize the qualities of good leadership, especially with the administrative aspects of the task in mind. In doing so, I unashamedly poach from the writings of Kouzes and Posner, which I commend to you.

First, they set out what they call the five practices of leadership,[11] all of which we see in Joshua. Leaders, they say,

1. model the way
2. inspire a shared vision
3. challenge the process
4. enable others to act
5. encourage the heart.

They then explore what people most look for in a leader, and say that research shows this 'has been pretty constant over time'.[12] So what are the qualities people want to see?

1. Honesty 'emerges as the single most important factor'.[13]
2. A forward-looking stance, which does not mean 'the magical power of a prescient visionary. The reality is more down-to-earth. It is the ability to imagine or discover a desirable destination toward which the company or agency, congregation or community should head.'[14]
3. Inspiration. 'People expect their leaders to be enthusiastic, energetic and positive about their future.'[15]
4. Competence, which is marked by 'relevant experience and sound judgment' and has 'the ability to get things done'.[16]

They conclude, 'Credibility is the foundation of leadership.'[17] Then they come up with two laws. Law 1: 'If you don't believe in the messenger, you won't believe the message.'[18] Law 2: DWYSYWD, that is, 'Do what you say you will do.'[19] Simple, isn't it! Except that we know leadership is anything but simple.

Joshua exemplifies all of this, and we'd be wise to do so as well.

Questions for reflection

1. How much do I value the gift of administration and see its importance?
2. Do I display administrative gifts? If so, what other kinds of gifts do I need to complement me? If not, how can I ensure appropriate administration is catered for?
3. Would people say I display the qualities found in good administrators, especially that of 'do what you say you will do' (DWYSYWD)?

19. Honour others (Joshua 14:6–14)

It may be only a small episode, but it opens a window on to something that can enhance or diminish a person's leadership. When the fighting was done and the division of the land had begun, Joshua honoured Caleb. We do not know what words were said, but we know it was a clear recognition by Joshua of the contribution Caleb had made to conquering the land.

The recognition took two forms. First, 'Joshua blessed Caleb.' That means more than that Joshua passed on his thanks and best wishes to him. Blessing 'is a rich one in biblical thought' and a means of effectively conveying God's abundant goodness and life-giving power on people.[1] Second, Joshua granted Caleb the city of Hebron as his possession. This city, which had long since been associated with the patriarchs, lay in the hill country some twenty miles south-west of Jerusalem and had earlier been conquered by Caleb himself.[2] So it was a fitting reward for his service.

Joshua and the importance of being secure

There is so much about Caleb that demands attention in its own right. His own rich testimony shows him to be a model of serving God wholeheartedly (verse 8), a claim endorsed by the writer of Joshua (verse 14). It showed him to be a faithful believer who held on to God's promises for a long period of time before seeing them fulfilled (verse 10). And it showed him to be as vigorous in serving God in his old age as he had been when much younger (verse 10). What a wonderful model he proves to be.

But our interest lies in Joshua's relationship with Caleb and what it teaches us about leadership. This relationship went back many decades, not least to when they memorably shared in the espionage mission which Moses sent out, and stood together, alone, against the majority of their fellow spies whose report discouraged the children of Israel from moving forwards in faith to conquer the land.[3]

Both men were obviously promising young leaders, and it would have been easy for them to become rivals. Did Joshua ever feel threatened by Caleb? Did Caleb ever feel jealous of Joshua and his prominence? Scripture gives no hint of this. As they meet now in their old age for Joshua to honour Caleb, they do so as companions, not as competitors; as those who had fought on the same side for the same cause, and not those who had fought each other.

This suggests that Joshua was secure in his own skin, secure enough to honour someone who had exhibited many of the qualities he himself possessed, and who could have been the leader of Israel instead of him without any reservation. Good leaders are those who are secure in their own gifts and calling. Insecure leaders can, by contrast, feel the need to prove themselves, and one of the ways of doing this is to adopt a competitive spirit that puts rivals down, points out their weaknesses and fails to recognize their successes. Joshua is free from any such defect, and so is able to acknowledge others.

A particular challenge in this area is the recognition a leader gives to his or her predecessor (something we touched on earlier). Leaders can be so keen to move on to a new age that they ignore the work done by their predecessor (or predecessors) on which they are building. Others may feel that their predecessors messed up or stayed past their point of effectiveness, and so maintain a noticeable silence about them, which achieves nothing except to feed suspicions or erode loyalties. Reflecting on Joshua's relationship with his great predecessor, Moses, we're reminded of the Blackabys' comment[4] that 'you can tell a lot about leaders by watching how they handle the ghosts of their predecessors'.[5] People soon pick up on whether a leader is generous or mean, secure or anxious, clear-sighted or prejudiced, relaxed or paranoid, from the way they honour those who have gone before them as well as those who are still around them.

Joshua and the importance of gratitude

Thanking others is an important part of the leader's task. If people feel they are being used and are underappreciated, they will perform less well than if they are genuinely valued. But we thank them not in order to make them more productive, but because it is right to do so. When answering the question, 'What is leadership?', Max De Pree, one of America's most successful Christian businessmen, begins his response like this: 'The first responsibility of a leader is to define reality. The last is to say thank you.'[6] Many leaders start well, but forget to complete the circle by expressing gratitude.

Kouzes and Posner provide some helpful practical advice about the art of being grateful. They begin exploring the topic by quoting Mary Le, of Intel Corporation, who warned, 'Recognition is important, challenging, and easily forgotten – so pay attention and don't forget to say "thanks".'[7] They go on to say that the most common complaint they hear 'about recognition is that far too often it's highly predictable, routine, and impersonal. A one-size-fits-all approach to recognition feels disingenuous, forced and thoughtless. Over time, it can even increase cynicism and actually damage credibility.'[8] If a group always acknowledges someone with the gift of a token from the local garden centre, whether they have a garden or only a window box, whether they like gardening or hate it, it soon becomes a hollow gesture!

So they recommend that leaders personalize recognition, which, we might note, is exactly what Joshua did for Caleb in giving him Hebron. They suggest this requires that:

- we get close to people;
- we are creative about our incentives;
- we learn that just saying 'thank you' can go a long way; and
- we are thoughtful about what will make the occasion memorable for the person we seek to honour.[9]

The cost of honouring others

Perhaps there is one more thing to add. Expressing thanks to others can sometimes highlight the loneliness of leadership. I recall a Christmas event at my son's junior school where the head teacher generously thanked all her staff, after which the pupils presented their classroom teachers with Christmas gifts. The teachers were laden! But I noticed the head standing to one side, alone. No-one gave her any gifts. They acknowledged the contribution of those they were closest to and most familiar with. They did not see the immense work that went on, a little removed, in the head's office, enabling the classroom teachers to be effective and consequently appreciated. I noticed it on that occasion because I've often noticed it elsewhere. Leadership can be lonely when leaders always seem to be those thanking others, and no-one ever seems to thank them but just take their work for granted. But then, this is perhaps a surprising application of Max De Pree's dictum: 'Leaders don't inflict pain. They bear pain.'[10] We might say, 'Leaders don't receive thanks. They give it.'

Honouring others can create a positive and wholesome environment that makes people keen to participate and spurs them on to better things. Don't think it is incidental or unimportant. Learn to say 'thank you' as creatively, genuinely and frequently as you can.

Questions for reflection

1. Do I view other leaders as potential threats and competitors or as valued colleagues? How secure am I in 'my own skin'?
2. How eager am I to honour others?
3. How often do I express gratitude to others, and do I do so creatively?

20. Display compassion (Joshua 20:1 – 21:45)

Our God is a compassionate God. As soon as the main settlement of the tribes has taken place, Joshua provides us with two pieces of evidence to support that claim, should we need them. There are two footnotes, as it were, to which Joshua needs to give attention, at God's command, before the task of allocation is complete.

The first (20:1–9) is that he is to set apart six cities, geographically spread out, to which those who 'accidentally and unintentionally' kill someone may escape and find a place of refuge. This was intended to put a stop to unjustified blood vengeance and ensure that true justice took place. Once the person had proved their innocence in a court, or once the current high priest died, they would be free to return home.

The second footnote (21:1–45) and the final act of allocation was the designation of forty-eight cities in which the otherwise landless tribe of Levites could live.[1] These were extracted from the territory belonging to the other tribes and scattered throughout the land, providing the Levites with 'pasture-lands for their livestock'.

Both of these are acts of compassion and thoughtfulness towards the plight of those who might be harshly dealt with by others. They are the sort of acts that any credible leader, and certainly any godly leader, needs to undertake.

Joshua as an emotionally intelligent leader

In taking these decisions, Joshua opens a window on to an aspect of leadership that has recently received a great deal of prominence: that of emotional intelligence (EI). This is a huge topic, and we are only going to consider one aspect of it, but let me set it in context. Good leaders need not only technical skill and analytical competence, but emotional intelligence as well. The possession of emotional intelligence, according to Daniel Goleman, is what 'distinguishes great leaders from merely good ones'.[2] In fact, he calculated that emotional intelligence was 'twice as important' as technical skills or IQ, 'for jobs at all levels'.[3] The absence of emotional intelligence inevitably restricts one's ability to lead, however gifted a leader may be in other areas.

Goleman posits that emotional intelligence consists of five different elements, namely, self-awareness, self-regulation, motivation, empathy and social skill.

Our interest lies in the fourth aspect of emotional intelligence, that of 'empathy'.[4] To be empathetic is to understand people's emotional make-up, and to consider their feelings when making decisions. It means that leaders will see things from the viewpoint of those they lead, and will not only hear the words they say, but be 'attuned to subtleties in body language' and sensitive to cultural, ethnic, gender and class differences. Every leader knows what it is like to secure verbal agreement in a meeting only to have it undermined in conversation or by non-compliance afterwards. Without employing emotional intelligence, decisions can be built on shaky foundations. Winning a vote needs to be accompanied by winning hearts.

Equally, all wise leaders who have any awareness of emotional intelligence know that not everyone will be as committed to the task, sold out on the goal, or as focused on winning the battle as they are. People will bring a host of their own concerns and issues to the table. And they don't always behave in rational ways, because they are not disembodied minds, but complex and emotional beings who live in a network of conflicting relationships, interests and ambitions. At the heart of emotional intelligence lies the need to consider the feelings of those we lead.

That's exactly what Joshua does, at the Lord's prompting, when he designates the cities of refuge and sets aside towns for the Levites.

The lack of emotional intelligence

Older schools of leadership and management often emphasized the 'hard skills of leadership', such as goal-setting, micro-measuring productivity, and drivenness. By any standard, Margaret Thatcher was one of the greatest leaders of recent times, whether one agreed with the direction of her leadership or not. She could demonstrate extraordinary emotional intelligence on a personal level and, never forgetting her own background, an extraordinary feel for ordinary housewives. But for a considerable time at least, she was old school as far as leadership was concerned towards those who worked closely with her.

On one occasion Sir John Hoskyns, the head of her Policy Unit and a trusted advisor, wrote her a 'blockbuster' and blistering memo on her style of leadership. He told her that her 'credibility and prestige were draining away very fast', and that she risked an internal revolt because her leadership style was wrong and she lacked management competence. He wrote,

> You break every rule of good man-management. You bully your weaker colleagues. You criticise colleagues in front of their officials. They can't answer back without appearing to be disrespectful, in front of others to a woman and to a Prime Minister. You abuse the situation. You give little praise or credit, and you are too ready to blame others when things go wrong . . . *The result . . . is an unhappy ship.* This demoralisation is hidden only from you.

He urged her to '*Lead by encouragement, not criticism*', adding,

> Churchill provided the element of will and courage, as you do, without which nothing could have been achieved. But when the Battle of Britain was over, he gave *all* the credit to others. You must make the members of your team feel ten feet tall, not add to their fears and self-doubts. Say 'we', not 'I'.[5]

To what extent Mrs Thatcher changed her style of leadership as a result of the memo is debatable. She did not discuss it with its author, as he requested, subsequently saying to him only, 'I got your letter. No one has ever written like that to a prime minister before.'[6] Their working relationship was often uneasy from then on, until Hoskyns moved from his post a year later.

Emotional intelligence: Joshua had it; Mrs Thatcher didn't, at least not to start with. Jesus had an abundance of it, aided, no doubt, by his divine status. John tells us on several occasions about Jesus' ability to 'read' people. It was evident when he met Nathanael.[7] Referring to the state of people's hearts and minds, John tells us that Jesus 'knew all people'[8] and could tell those who didn't believe in him and the one who would betray him 'from the first'.[9] More generally, he could connect with a wide range of people, and it is evident that he knew their needs and whether they were genuinely open to God's grace, in which case he showed sensitivity and compassion to them, or were arrogant in their resistance to God, in which case he could stand firm against them.

Great leaders need EI. However correct their leadership may be according to the textbooks, without it, people will think of it as if they are painting by numbers, doing the correct things but devoid of any personal heart. It's worth getting others to rate you on the EI scale, and if you don't rate highly, get experienced people around you to school you in it, mentor you and challenge you about it. Cultivate EI for all it's worth. It is a prize worth more than the successful accomplishment of any task or goal. It not only produces better results and easier working relationships but, and this is the most significant thing, mirrors the style and compassion of the Lord whom we serve.

Questions for reflection

1. Am I sensitive to the needs and situations of others? Am I an over-demanding, self-absorbed leader?
2. How would I grade myself on the empathy scale?
3. Would others say I possess 'emotional intelligence'?

21. Guard unity (Joshua 22:1–34)

No sooner had the settlement of the Promised Land been completed than an event occurred which threatened to wreck the whole project. The actions of the two-and-a-half tribes that had been permitted to settle east of Jordan endangered the unity of Israel, so it looked as if their embryonic nationhood was to be fractured before it had really begun.

This is exactly the kind of unexpected situation that leaders walk into, often through no fault of their own. Conflict arises, and unity can easily be imperilled for apparently 'innocent' or trivial reasons. It is the task of a leader to find a way through and preserve the unity of God's people, unless, that is, the very core of the gospel is at stake, as it was in Galatia.[1] Joshua 22 is a masterclass in how to ensure that we guard unity.

The story is told in five movements.

Joshua issues a wise warning (verses 1–9)

When the time came for the soldiers from the tribes of Reuben, Gad and the half-tribe of Manasseh to return to their families east of the River Jordan, Joshua commended them for their participation in the war to conquer Canaan, and for their standing with the other tribes until the task had been completed. Having done so, he told them they could go home to their families, but he sent them off with a warning to 'be very careful to keep the commandment and the law that Moses the servant of the LORD gave you: to love the LORD your God, to walk in obedience to him, to keep his commands, to hold fast to him and to serve him with all your heart and with all your soul' (verse 5). So Joshua's pithy 'well done' was accompanied by an equally pithy 'watch out'.

In view of what was to happen, his words were to prove ironic. Having been commended for their solidarity with the rest of Israel, their actions were almost immediately to threaten division within Israel. Having been warned to be totally obedient, their actions were initially judged to be patent disobedience to the Lord.

The eastern tribes engage in questionable action (verse 10)

What happened? What was the problem?

Trouble started before they'd even got home. When they reached Geliloth before they crossed over the Jordan, they 'built an imposing altar there'. As we later discover, their intentions were good, but that was not how the western tribes interpreted their action. The law of Moses had made it crystal clear that worship was to be centralized at one altar, to ensure that God alone was to be worshipped and as a sign of unity among the tribes.[2]

David Howard suggests that they built an imposing altar there because its location on the 'mainland' rather than on the eastern bank of the Jordan was meant to indicate that they belonged to one united people, and that it was built on a grand scale so that it could be seen from their eastern homeland and would not be forgotten.[3] However, whatever their intention might have been, their action was misinterpreted by the majority tribes, who regarded it as an act of disobedience and rebellion. This is a classic case of what has come to be known as the law of unintended consequences, which states that the *unintended* consequences of any action often outweigh the *intended* consequences.[4] In doing anything, we need to see how our actions will be understood by others, insofar as we can, since others may well see them in a very different light from us. The eastern tribes failed to take that into account.

Israel responds with foolish impetuosity (verses 11–20)

The immediate reaction of the main tribes was to hold an assembly at Shiloh and plan for war. Shiloh was where the tabernacle was located,[5] and was meant to be the one place of worship at this stage in Israel's history. The hawks were very much in the ascendency. They did not stop to enquire or consider whether the erection of the altar could be seen in a different light or not. They adopted the speedy logic of condemnation. They assumed that the altar was built for worship, that the worship would be impure, and therefore the action was divisive and their faith apostate. Let's go and sort them out! Suspicion reigned, and trust never entered their heads.

The philosopher Onora O'Neill devoted her 2002 Reith Lectures to the breakdown of trust in contemporary society. Because she thought the issue more complex than the popular newspapers did, she argued, 'We may not have evidence for a crisis of trust; but we have massive evidence of a culture of suspicion.'[6] The years since she delivered those lectures have

provided massively increasing evidence for her thesis in the
public sphere and, sadly, the church is by no means immune
from the malady of mistrust and suspicion either.

In this war-mongering atmosphere they decided to send a
delegation to talk to their eastern neighbours. It consisted of
ten heavyweight men and was headed by Phinehas. Now, if
you know anything about Phinehas, you may not find that
piece of information encouraging. He had once killed an
Israelite man and a Midianite woman with one spear because
of their sexual immorality.[7] He had proved himself zealous
to defend God's honour, and wasn't likely to accept anything
that seemed to deviate one iota from the law of Moses. But
at least their decision meant the issue was going to be dealt
with face to face, rather than at a distance or by relying on
mere rumour.

When the delegation arrived, their questioning was all
based on the assumption of guilt. There was no such thing in
their minds as being innocent before being proved guilty. It
was 'How could you break faith . . . ? How could you turn
away from the Lord . . . in rebellion? Was not the sin of Peor
enough for us?' Their language was far from moderate. They
spoke of rebellion, of defiling the land, of selfishness, of
unfaithfulness and of God's anger. The delegation did nothing
to alleviate the crisis and everything to fuel it.

The eastern tribes provide a considered response
(verses 21–29)

Fortunately, the eastern tribes kept their cool and did not
prove defensive. Their response was a model of humility and
reason as they met the stoked-up delegation. They explained
that they were not guilty of any of the things of which they
were being accused. Rather than their altar being a hasty or

rebellious action, they had carefully worked things out before building it.

First, they explained, they had worked it out before the Lord (verses 22–23)

They had a huge reverence for the Lord, whom they acknowledged as 'The Mighty One'. They were very conscious that they were accountable to him. If they had done wrong, they pleaded, 'may the LORD himself call us to account'.

Second, they had worked it out for their context (verses 24–25)

Looking to the future, they feared that the solidarity they currently enjoyed might not last, and that sometime in the future the descendants of the majority tribes would cut them off from their membership in the elect people. They feared that the porous boundary between them would, with time, become a rigid barrier. Easy access would be denied, and the tribes would separate. They built the altar precisely in order to promote loyalty and preserve unity, not to foster division.

Third, they had also worked it out in the light of the law (verses 26–29)

They knew that the law forbade the building of a sacrificial altar, so they had not built an altar on which to offer sacrifices. They had built one to perpetuate memory.[8] Onora O'Neill insightfully argues that you cannot have trust without a corresponding trustworthiness. 'We fantasise,' she says, 'irresponsibly that we promulgate rights without thinking carefully about the counterpart obligations.'[9] But you can't have rights without responsibilities. The eastern tribes knew that. They knew there was one altar on which burnt offerings and other offerings were to be offered, and it wasn't theirs. As we noted earlier, they were committed to continuing to worship at the tabernacle, then located at Shiloh (verse 29).

The tribes reach a satisfactory conclusion (verses 30–34)

The situation was soon resolved, with both sides playing their part in lowering the temperature and bringing healing to their fractured relationships. The eastern tribes, as we have seen, set out a considered reason for their action that proved their loyalty. Would that all who cause potential conflict in the church could learn from them. Too often the issues of disagreement are not well founded, as here, on Scripture and reason. All too often, the cause is emotional and unthinking, prejudiced, and built, if at all, on a very shaky foundation in Scripture.

The delegation's role in reaching a satisfactory resolution was simple, although it is extraordinary how difficult we find it today to practise what they did. First, they listened (verse 30). Having set out their case, they permitted the eastern tribes time to explain themselves thoroughly, and they paid careful attention to what they said. Active listening is a demanding discipline. Too often we're not really listening to others because we think we know what they're going to say! Alternatively, some of us think it clever to adopt the stance of media interviewers who bamboozle and interrupt interviewees with another question before they have allowed them a few words in response to the question they've just asked. Many conflicts could be resolved if we cultivated the skill of actively listening to each other.

The delegation not only listened to the eastern tribes, but also accepted their explanation with good grace (verses 30–31). They did not pass a cautious verdict, full of mental reservation;

they affirmed the faithfulness of the eastern tribes and the presence of the Lord in the conversation. Then they turned the conversation Godwards and praised him for preventing war and reconciling them to each other (verses 32–33). The memory of the episode was sealed and perpetuated by the altar that had been the cause of tension, and they renamed it as a witness to their united faithfulness to the Lord their God (verse 34).

Listen and learn

Since the church we are called to lead is not yet perfect, conflicts, tensions and potential divisions will sadly arise. When they do, we have an obligation to work to preserve its unity. There are resources which are helpful in guiding us to do that, but this incident provides us with some important starting points. Reviewing it, we learn:

- to acknowledge people's contribution, as Joshua did in dismissing the eastern tribes;
- to apply preventative medicine, as he did in warning them of potential future risks;
- to avoid precipitate responses, especially if built on false assumptions;
- to deal with issues face to face;
- to listen to all sides carefully;
- to accept other people's integrity unless there is clear reason not to do so; and
- to find the Lord in the midst of the mess and draw people back to what is essential.

It is the obligation of Christian leadership to 'make every effort to keep the unity of the Spirit through the bond of peace'.[10]

Questions for reflection

1. What issues are potentially divisive in the group I lead?
2. How good am I at listening to those who seem to be behaving unacceptably, with a view to perhaps understanding their motives better?
3. What is my approach to conflict resolution?

22. Mentor others (Joshua 23:1–16)

For all Joshua's brilliance as a leader, he was not perfect. Perhaps his biggest weakness, as mentioned in the Introduction, was his failure, as far as we can tell, to mentor a younger generation of leaders who would succeed him. We can sometimes learn as effectively from an example of poor practice as we can from examples of good practice, and here we learn from what Joshua failed to do rather than from what he did.

Joshua as a collaborative leader

Joshua was certainly a team player and collaborative leader. He was not the lone ranger who performed a solo act. As we come to the end of his story, we see him addressing all Israel, paying special attention to 'the elders, leaders, judges and officials' (verse 2). These people had constantly been at his side.[1] Eleazar, Aaron's son and successor as high priest, is also referred to on a number of occasions as playing a significant role in the settlement process.[2] And as mentioned in the last chapter, Phinehas, his son, came to the fore as the leader of the delegation to the Transjordan tribes when things threatened to fall apart. So Joshua certainly knew how to be a team player.

We only pick up the merest of hints about how they worked together. It seems to have been a harmonious team since we never hear of any rivalry or plots to unseat Joshua, even though they were quite different in role and almost certainly in personality too. Eleazar represented the established priestly leadership of Israel. Joshua represented the charismatic lay leadership of Israel. They entered their offices in different ways: Eleazar by assuming the high priestly vestments, Joshua through an endowment of the Spirit.[3] On a couple of occasions people went to Eleazar with their requests rather than directly to Joshua.[4] Perhaps Eleazar was a more approachable person, but that's reading more into the text than we are told. Both incidents related to settlement issues, and Eleazar had had major responsibilities in that.

Joshua seems to have been careful to take the main leaders into his confidence first, and then depend on them to execute his orders and disseminate his decisions throughout the camp. Drawing people into the inner circle like this will often keep them on board. People in general, but leaders in particular, become disaffected when they are left out in the cold and don't know what is going on. Leadership tasks seem to have been allocated well, and careful lines of demarcation drawn.

The most beneficial leadership team

No leader is self-sufficient, and the development of a team that is comfortable working together is another of the leader's primary responsibilities. Commenting on the performance of

Leicester City (my local team!) in a recent newspaper article, Matthew Syed reported on a wide range of research, from medicine to aviation, to show how performance was greatly enhanced by a team working cooperatively together, in 'shared decision-making and a collective response to crises' rather than by relying on a star performer, however eminent. He wrote:

> Almost every branch of human endeavour is discovering, in different ways, that in situations of complexity, it is not the ability of individuals that matters so much as how they co-ordinate. This is not to say that individual skill is not important. Rather it is to say historically – in everything from the military, to hospitals, to sport – we have put precious little thought into the subtle mechanisms that turn talented soloists into an orchestra.

Even improvised jazz, he says, is a complex network of musicians playing together, where 'the note of any one player only makes sense if other players are playing in harmony'.[5] There are certainly lessons here, especially for churches which have relied on 'solo ministries' or single charismatic leaders. Teams matter. But what sort of teams?

Every team needs a balance of skills, and it is exactly the same whether it is football or church.[6] Alex Ferguson states the obvious when he writes, 'Balance is the key to every team. It is impossible to win with eleven goalkeepers or with a group of people with identical talents. I imagine that's true in other organizations too.'[7] Later he adds, 'Every member of the team has got to understand that they are part of the jigsaw puzzle . . .'[8] Team members who act as lone rangers are as unhelpful, undermining and potentially destructive as the leader him- or herself would be if acting alone.

We are all different, and if we can learn to complement each other, we can derive tremendous strength from collaborative team leadership. If we misunderstand each other or become competitive, the team becomes dysfunctional and will never achieve its goals. Bob Phillips has helpfully and entertainingly set out what roles people need to adopt on leadership teams, and how four different types of people are usually required in order to be effective.[9] The leaders differ from each other according to their place on two axes. One axis is the ask–tell axis; the other is the task–people axis. Teams need people in each resulting quadrant. They need:

- drivers, who are task-oriented and tell others what to do;
- analytics, who are also task-oriented but ask questions about the task;
- amiables, who are people-oriented and ask questions of others; and
- expressives, who are also people-oriented but provide information, often in a colourful way.

Drivers are often best in the leadership chair. They are decisive, concerned with the big picture and keen to see action. Analytics are often the administrators, managers, lawyers and accountants, who seek to ensure that it is possible to translate the vision into reality. Amiables have good relations with people, and are liked and trusted by them. They can be vital in encouraging people to change, and in smoothing over feathers that decisions may have ruffled. Expressives are good communicators and can convey a message about a decision or change, and get people on board by presenting an inspiring message about the future. As far as character goes, they all have different strengths and weaknesses. None is spiritually superior to the others. Each plays to certain strengths and allows the display of a set of virtues. But each also presents its own particular set of temptations. It's playing as a team that secures the victories.

Joshua's failure to mentor

The importance of mentoring

While we get a picture of Joshua as a collaborative leader, we never get a picture of him as a mentor of a younger generation of leaders. He works well with his peers, but if he was committed to developing the next generation of leaders, the book that bears his name is remarkably silent about it. This is surprising in view of the close and beneficial mentoring he himself had received from Moses. We can only speculate as to why he did not give himself to this task, as we have no inkling as to why he didn't do so. Perhaps he was just too busy!

Of course, absence of evidence is not evidence of absence. It may well be that he did it, but we're just not told. But what happened to Israel after Joshua's day lends support to the view that it was just not something he gave his energies to. For then Israel tragically fell apart, and lack of leadership was a major factor in its doing so. It lurched from one crisis to another as God graciously raised up short-term leaders who were one-offs in more than one sense. They rescued Israel from their enemies and put them back on the right track for a time, before the people descended into the next disaster, and the whole cycle repeated itself. The book of Judges underlines the vital importance of training the next generation of leaders.

Bill Hybels writes passionately about the importance of mentoring: 'Whatever challenges our churches face in the years ahead, I hope we can face with confidence, knowing that we were wise enough to invest in the next generation of leaders. There is nothing that seasoned leaders can do that can have more impact than that.'[10] I fully agree.

The meaning of mentoring

The words 'mentor' and 'mentoring' have become buzzwords in recent decades. Mentoring covers a range of activity, and any mentoring relationship needs to be clear about expectations. At one end of the spectrum it can be akin to offering spiritual direction and involve deep challenges about our interior life and motives. Somewhere in the middle it can involve being a general life companion or guide, with the mentor reflecting generally and widely on the direction and progress of life. At the other end of the spectrum it can be about serving as a coach in terms of specific skills, such as leadership – it's widely used in business in this way – or preaching.

Assuming our concern is about developing Christian leaders, we envisage that mentoring will cover a balance and range of issues:

- The spiritual dimension. Is our mentoree (to use an ugly word!) growing as a disciple of Jesus, and how is their walk with God? Do they know the Bible? Are there persistent sins that are likely to become fatal flaws? What is their relationship to the church?
- The personal dimension. Are they emotionally stable? Are they secure in themselves? Are there personality weaknesses, such as arrogance or false humility, which need attention? What are the strengths, as well as the weaknesses, of their

character? What are their relationships like? Are they faithful to their family, accepting responsibility for their role as partner or parent? Are they respected? If not, why not? Are they reliable? Are they intelligent, by which I don't mean academic intelligence necessarily, but do they cotton on to things? Can they handle money?

- The leadership dimension. Here one thinks more particularly about the skills required of leaders and the tasks they undertake. The mentor will seek to develop a keen leadership eye, build in good practices and review bad ones, with a view to avoiding them.

It's obvious from this that the nature of the relationship between the mentor and mentoree is fundamental to its success.[11] Mutual trust, openness and respect are essential. James Lawrence highlights this when he says his 'favoured definition' is that 'Christian mentoring is a dynamic, intentional relationship of trust in which one person (mentor) enables another (mentoree) to maximize the grace of God in their life through the Holy Spirit, in the service of God's kingdom purposes, by sharing their life, experience and resources'.[12] 'Relationship', 'trust', 'dynamic' and 'intentional' are the key words.

Reviewing the mentoring relationship
The quality of the relationship needs to be honestly assessed and monitored. If the chemistry isn't there and it isn't going to work, it's worth not getting into it in the first place, or calling it a day if you've already started. How close and open should the relationship be? People will benefit from different levels of intensity, depending on their own personalities and

security. On the spectrum of mentoring relationships, where does this relationship fall? Is it definitely one of teacher or expert to pupil or novice, or more towards being peers on a journey together? Is the mentor a role model or a fellow explorer? Is the mentoree in awe of the mentor? If so, that is an unhealthy learning environment, since we grow through critically evaluating what we're taught. Respect, yes. Awe, no. Alternatively, is the mentoree in fear of the mentor? Well, that's not a good learning environment either, and not likely to produce growth in the mentoree. Has the mentoree a healthy, but not uncritical, respect for the mentor? That's the best sort of relationship to have.

'Change,' says James Lawrence, 'is at the centre of a mentoring relationship; growth is involved.'[13] You are not meeting just because you enjoy each other's company or to have a cosy chat, but in order to enable growth to take place. You have an agenda, one that you should both agree. That will sometimes mean teaching new things, but more often mentoring will mean learning from experience by reviewing situations and giving feedback.

Intentionality is vital. Without it, a mentoring relationship goes nowhere and achieves nothing. Intentionality involves thinking clearly about expectations. What does a mentoree want to get out of the relationship, and can the mentor deliver it? How often are you going to meet? How formal or informal is the mentoring going to be? And for how long? That's a question that needs answering both for individual meetings and in terms of how many months or years this specific relationship lasts.

The good mentor is never more delighted than when their mentoree outshines them and goes beyond them in the leadership they exercise or the particular field of ministry that has been the focus of the relationship.

Conclusion

All young leaders should be encouraged to find a good mentor. But they should also be encouraged to mentor others. They need not wait until they achieve a certain level of seniority, since not only will they already be further down the path of experience than the younger leaders coming up behind them, but most of us would testify that we learn so much as we teach others. Their mentoring will be much more of the 'exploring together' type than the 'experienced teacher helping the unlearned pupil' type. But the relationship will still pay dividends.

Paul sets out both the right approach and the standard required when he writes of his relationship with the fledgling church of Thessalonica: 'We cared for you. Because we loved you so much, we were delighted to share with you not only the gospel of God but our lives as well.'[14] It requires nothing short of an opening up of oneself and a sharing of one's life and experience with those we seek to develop in leadership.

The biggest mistake Joshua made in his leadership, it would seem, was a failure to develop leaders who would follow him. Let's not make the same mistake. The controversial politician Enoch Powell once said, 'All political lives, unless they are cut off in midstream at a happy juncture, end in failure, because that is the nature of politics and of human affairs.' Reviewing recent history suggests he was right. But by the grace of God, what's true in politics isn't true in the church. One way to guarantee that it's not true of us and our years in leadership is to leave a legacy of others who will not only follow in our footsteps – albeit in different-sized shoes! – but walk in those footsteps better than we would ever have done ourselves.

Questions for reflection

1. Where do I position myself on a scale of 1 to 10, where 1 stands for solo leadership and 10 for being fully a team player?
2. Am I essentially a driver, an analytic, an amiable or an expressive? Have I taken steps to ensure those around me complement my primary leadership orientation with different orientations? Or have I surrounded myself with people just like me?
3. Do I have a vision for mentoring the next generation of leaders? If so, who am I mentoring and how am I putting this vision into practice?

23. Keep focus (Joshua 24:1–28)

It is one thing to conquer the land, but 'it is another to maintain the vigour and vision over the long haul in order to complete the conquest and preserve its results'.[1] Winning the battle is one thing; winning the peace another. Joshua had led his people to victory and had successfully settled the tribes in their allocated territories. But what next?

Joshua and the challenge of success

The successful leader faces two challenges: perseverance and mission drift. In his farewell speech, delivered just before his death at the age of 110, Joshua reveals himself to have been aware of both challenges. Consequently, 'after a long time had passed' and they had enjoyed many years of rest from their enemies,[2] Joshua called an assembly of the leaders and people of Israel so that they could renew their covenant to the Lord. The most dangerous thing of all would have been to take the people's covenant loyalty for granted. It would have been a dereliction of an important aspect of the duty of leadership. In acting as he did, Joshua consciously brings to their minds the loyalty they owe to the covenant God and, in so doing, purposefully rejuvenates their sense of identity.

So much of what we have learned about Joshua and his skills in leadership and communication reach their climax here. Look at how he addresses his people:

He recalls their story (verses 1–13)

We noted the importance of that earlier in chapter 7. To be accurate, it is not so much their story as God's story. Preaching on this a century ago, F. B. Meyer pointed out that 'throughout the story, the entire stress is laid on the grace of God. *I* took; *I* gave; *I* sent; *I* brought; *I* destroyed; *I* gave; *I* delivered. Not a mention is made of Israel's mighty men. All is attributed to the ultimate sources of nature, history and grace – the supreme will of God.'[3] It is not only telling the story, but the way we tell it, that matters.

He issues a challenge (verses 14–15)

Joshua is not interested in giving them a history lesson for its own sake. He is leading them to a point of seeing what has shaped them, and the implication for their own day. Will they fear the Lord who rescued them from the Egyptians, or is that 'undesirable' to them? If so, are they going to turn to worship the local gods?

He sets an example (verse 15b)

He firmly nails his own colours, and those of his family, to the mast: 'But as for me and my household, we will serve the LORD.' Others may choose the path of unfaithfulness, but he will remain undeviatingly loyal to the God who has been their Saviour and Lord.

He probes their understanding (verses 16–22)

Aware of the heightened emotions that such large gatherings can generate and the all-too-easy promises made on such occasions, when the people say, 'Of course, we too will serve the LORD', Joshua doesn't accept their initial response without question. Did he detect some insincerity in their reply? He pushes them so that they understand the immensity of their commitment. 'Do they realize,' he counters, 'their inability to serve such a holy and jealous God and how high the stakes are if they renege on their promise?' Unlike other deities, God demands exclusive and absolute devotion. They had grasped his grace, but did they also grasp the complementary aspects of his nature, that he was a jealous God who made 'stringent demands'?[4] They seem somewhat casual about it and oblivious to their own inadequacies and inability to deliver on their promise, as if their words are sufficient in themselves to carry them forwards to obedience.[5] They do not express their need of God until Joshua pushes them further. Nonetheless, they say they understand what he is asking and repeat their commitment to serve the Lord.

He spells out the implications (verses 23–24)

Still Joshua has not finished with them. He will not permit them to indulge in cheap promises or bargain-basement spirituality. 'If you really mean it,' he goes on, 'then get rid of the foreign gods, eject their idols from your homes, and totally surrender yourself to the Lord.' Total surrender usually has some very practical implications for the reordering of one's life. The people affirm that that is their intention.

He seals their promise (verses 25–28)

Joshua recorded the event so that there could be no possible doubt as to what they had said that day. And as we have seen him do before, he then erected a memorial stone so that there was a tangible symbol of their commitment for all to see.

Joshua's carefully constructed address and the conversation that followed encouraged the people to keep going as loyal servants of God, whatever the future might hold. It also focused their minds on their unique and central calling, bringing them back to what was at the core of their faith. It sought to prevent mission drift.

The challenge of mission drift

What is it?

If perseverance is one of the most demanding challenges that leaders face, then mission drift is one of the most subtle. *Mission Drift* is the name of a research-based book that explores the common phenomenon of mission agencies and churches drifting away from their original purpose and calling. Such groups are particularly vulnerable to this often disguised and unrecognized temptation, having known some initial success. For example, mission agencies that began as evangelistic and church planting movements begin to adopt wider agendas, which eventually squeeze out the group's originating evangelistic purpose. The authors summarize their message: 'Too often, as Christian organizations grow, the Gospel often becomes cursory, expendable, or even forgotten. Again and again and again leaders have watched their ministries . . . professionalize, expand and lose sight of their original goals. Even churches can stray from their calling.'[6]

They write somewhat pessimistically,

Without careful attention, faith-based organizations
will inevitably drift from their founding mission.
It's that simple. It will happen.

Slowly, silently, and with little fanfare, organizations routinely drift from their original purpose, and most will never return to their original intent. It has happened repeatedly throughout history and it was happening to us.[7]

Reasons for it

Sometimes mission drift occurs as a deliberate result of decisions taken. It can be thought necessary for the remit of the group to be widened if it is to build on its success. So churches that are blessed with conversions often feel the pressure to engage with their community more and more, and so set up a number of community ministries. Unless all senses are alert, the church can drift into becoming a centre for social work rather than a centre of disciple making. There is a string of theological colleges and universities that illustrate this point. They began with a clear evangelical commitment to teach the Bible and then, in the interests of intellectual credibility, sought wider academic recognition and ended up broadening their approach and curriculum and relegating the teaching of the Bible altogether, let alone preserving an evangelical approach to it. These cases are well documented historically.

Another reason for mission drift is simply complacency. From his own experience as a hugely successful football manager, Alex Ferguson admitted that complacency 'can often start seeping into an organization that has a string of triumphs'.[8] Watch success! It can be a trap, as Joshua well knew.

Can it be avoided?

Greer and Horst recommend that every mission agency, church and charity needs to build in 'course correctors' to ensure that people know what their mission is, and appoint guardians who will hold people accountable so that they keep true to their calling. The assembly at Shechem was Joshua's 'course corrector', while his recording the event in 'the Book of the Law of God' and his setting up of the memorial stone were at least witnesses, if not exactly guardians, to the mission Israel agreed to there.

Ferguson's answer was to keep a sharp focus: 'I have yet to encounter anyone who has achieved massive success without closing themselves off from the demands of others and foregoing pastimes.'[9] Don't get sucked into a wide range of demands, however inviting, worthy or plausible, but be leaders with a single mind.

There is a sense in which Paul is addressing the issue of mission drift in his pastoral letters. They repay careful study from this perspective. Looking at 2 Timothy alone, remember how Paul tells Timothy to 'fan into flame' God's gift of the Spirit, received at the start of his ministry,[10] to guard the original gospel,[11] not to slack off,[12] to keep focus as a preacher of God's Word,[13] to avoid being sidetracked,[14] and to persevere in his original calling and the mission of the gospel,[15] and so much more.

Conclusion

We've travelled a long way in this book with Joshua, and he has been a great teacher, if not a perfect one, about leadership. Take note of what he teaches us about staving off mission drift, as much as what he has modelled and taught on other leadership issues. Protect yourself, your ministry, your church, your organization against mission drift with all the energy that God provides, so that you may not just begin well, but end well too, 'complet[ing] the ministry you have received in the Lord',[16] and at all times being careful to 'guard what has been entrusted to your care'.[17]

Questions for reflection

1. What do I take for granted in my relationship with God, especially if I have known some success in leadership?
2. Am I conscious of the danger of mission drift?
3. Reflecting on my leadership experience so far, can I detect any mission drift?
4. What practicable steps can I take to remain focused and prevent mission drift?

Notes

Introduction: Joshua 'in whom is the spirit of leadership'

1. Numbers 13:8; Joshua 1:1.
2. 1 Chronicles 7:27.
3. Numbers 13:8, 16. See further David M. Howard Jr, *Joshua*, New American Commentary (Broadman & Holman, 1998), pp. 73–74.
4. Moses is referred to as 'the servant of the LORD' fourteen times in Joshua, starting with Joshua 1:1. Joshua is only granted the title once, in 24:29.
5. Exodus 17:8–16.
6. Exodus 24:13; 33:11; Numbers 11:28.
7. Exodus 24:13; 32:17.
8. Exodus 33:7–11.
9. Deuteronomy 32:44.
10. Numbers 11:28.
11. Numbers 14:6, 30–38.
12. Numbers 27:18–23; Deuteronomy 31:7–8.
13. Deuteronomy 34:10–12.
14. Deuteronomy 3:28.
15. Deuteronomy 31:14, 23.

16. Numbers 27:18. The NIV includes the words 'of leadership' which other translations omit. The context amply justifies the inclusion of these additional words.
17. Deuteronomy 34:9.
18. Jeremiah 18:18.
19. The 'non-religious' words are *proistēmi* (Romans 12:8; 1 Thessalonians 5:12), meaning to be at the head of, to direct or lead; *kubernēsis* (1 Corinthians 12:28), referring to a pilot in command of steering a ship; and *hēgeomenōn* (Hebrews 13:7, 17, 24), which was used of military commanders, high officials and princely leaders.
20. Mark 10:45.
21. Romans 12:8.
22. Genesis 12:7.
23. Deuteronomy 18:18–20. The prophet like Moses was Jesus Christ.
24. Psalm 146:3.

1. Assume responsibility (Joshua 1:1–6)

1. A. Graeme Auld, *Joshua, Judges and Ruth*, Daily Study Bible (St Andrew Press, 1984), p. 7.
2. J. Oswald Sanders, *Spiritual Leadership* (Lakeland, 1967), p. 45. The exclusive language is one of several features that date the book, which is nevertheless still immensely worthwhile reading.
3. Alex Ferguson with Michael Moritz, *Leading* (Hodder & Stoughton, 2015), p. 313.
4. Ibid., p. 69.
5. Ibid.
6. Ibid., p. 367.
7. Rudolph W. Giuliani with Ken Kurson, *Leadership* (Little Brown, 2002), p. 69.

8. Ibid., p. 70.

9. 1 Corinthians 3:10–15.

10. 1 Corinthians 9:27.

11. 2 Corinthians 11:2.

12. Ephesians 5:27.

13. 1 Thessalonians 2:19; see also 2:7–13.

14. Ken Blanchard, *Leading at a Higher Level* (Pearson Education, 2010), p. 17.

15. David G. Firth, *The Message of Joshua*, The Bible Speaks Today (IVP, 2015), p. 33.

16. As Henry and Richard Blackaby write, 'You can tell a lot about leaders by watching how they handle the ghosts of their predecessors.' *Called to Be God's Leader: Lessons from the Life of Joshua* (Nelson, 2004), p. 49.

17. Matthew 28:20; Hebrews 13:5.

18. John 15:5.

19. David M. Howard Jr, *Joshua*, New American Commentary (Broadman & Holman, 1998), p. 45.

20. 2 Timothy 1:6–7.

21. See e.g. Lyle W. Dorsett, *A Passion for Souls: The Life of D. L. Moody* (Moody Press, 1997), pp. 274–277.

2. Build foundations (Joshua 1:7–9)

1. Ecclesiastes 10:10.

2. David M. Howard Jr, *Joshua*, New American Commentary (Broadman & Holman, 1998), p. 85. Howard points out that 'to obey' translates two Hebrew words that are paired thirty-nine times in the Old Testament to exhort people to keep the law.

3. David G. Firth, *The Message of Joshua*, The Bible Speaks Today (IVP, 2015), p. 37.

4. Ezra 7:10.

5. LeRoy Eims, *Be the Leader You Were Meant to Be* (Victor Books, 1975), p. 19.
6. To avoid any misunderstanding, the author trained as a sociologist and has taught sociology and used sociological insights during much of his ministry. So I am not opposed to using the insights of contemporary human sciences in principle. But all such tools need to be used with discernment and as supplementary, not superior, to the revelation of God.
7. Among the many illustrations of this trend, note the social gospel movement of the early twentieth century, the student movement in the mid-twentieth century and numerous evangelical movements that veer in a theologically liberal direction for the sake of winning converts. See further, Steve Bruce, *Firm in the Faith* (Gower, 1984) and Brian Stanley, *The Global Diffusion of Evangelicalism: The Age of Billy Graham and John Stott* (IVP Academic, 2013).
8. Exodus 32:1–33.
9. Exodus 33:3.
10. Exodus 33:5.
11. Exodus 33:15.
12. Joshua 2:24; 3:7, 10; 4:14; 6:27; 10:14, 42; 13:6; 14:12; 21:44; 23:3, 10.
13. John 5:30.
14. John 15:5.
15. Proverbs 3:5–7.
16. Alex Ferguson with Michael Moritz, *Leading* (Hodder & Stoughton, 2015), p. 49.

3. Make decisions (Joshua 1:10–17)

1. Walter C. Wright, *Relational Leadership: A Biblical Model for Leadership Service* (Paternoster, 2000), p. 187.
2. Numbers 32:1–42.

3. Numbers 32:28–30.

4. 1 Kings 12:1–24; 2 Chronicles 10:1 – 11:4.

5. James 3:17.

6. J. Oswald Sanders, *Spiritual Leadership* (Lakeland, 1967), pp. 66–67.

7. James M. Kouzes and Barry Z. Posner, *The Leadership Challenge*, 4th edn (Jossey-Bass, 2007), p. 58.

8. Wright, *Relational Leadership*, p. 187, the emphasis is Wright's.

4. Gather intelligence (Joshua 2:1–22)

1. Numbers 13:1 – 14:44.

2. David G. Firth, *The Message of Joshua*, The Bible Speaks Today (IVP, 2015), p. 45.

3. Trent C. Butler, *Joshua*, Word Biblical Commentary (Word, 1983), pp. 34–35.

4. Richard Baxter, *The Cure for Church Divisions* (1670), Clause 20.

5. Rudolph W. Giuliani with Ken Kurson, *Leadership* (Little Brown, 2002), p. 51.

6. Alex Ferguson with Michael Moritz, *Leading* (Hodder & Stoughton, 2015), p. 11.

7. Ibid., p. 66.

8. Ibid., p. 68.

5. Prepare thoroughly (Joshua 3:1–5)

1. David G. Firth, *The Message of Joshua*, The Bible Speaks Today (IVP, 2015), p. 55.

2. Joshua 3:3.

3. 2 Samuel 6:3–7.

4. Exodus 19:10, 14–15; Numbers 11:18.

5. Dale Ralph Davis, *Joshua*, Focus on the Bible (Christian Focus, 2000), p. 34.

6. Take risks (Joshua 3:6–17)

1. Cited in Peter Brierley, *Vision Building: Knowing Where You're Going* (Hodder & Stoughton, 1989), p. 186.
2. 2 Corinthians 4:18; Hebrews 11:1.
3. Gilbert Kirby, a minister of the Countess of Huntingdon's Connexion, was General Secretary of the Evangelical Alliance UK and subsequently Principal of London Bible College.
4. David G. Firth, *The Message of Joshua*, The Bible Speaks Today (IVP, 2015), p. 57.
5. See further, Dale Ralph Davis, *Joshua*, Focus on the Bible (Christian Focus, 2000), p. 35.
6. James M. Kouzes and Barry Z. Posner, *The Leadership Challenge*, 4th edn (Jossey-Bass, 2007), pp. 191, 193.

7. Recall history (Joshua 4:1 – 5:12)

1. M. H. Woudstra, *The Book of Joshua*, New International Commentary on the Old Testament (Eerdmans, 1981), p. 90.
2. Howard E. Gardner, *Leading Minds: An Anatomy of Leadership* (HarperCollins, 1996), pp. 9–10.
3. See e.g. Joshua 23 – 24.
4. Gardner, *Leading Minds*, pp. 10–11.
5. An extract from Barack Obama's victory speech delivered at Grant Park, Chicago, on 4 November 2008. See http://edition.cnn.com/2008/POLITICS/11/04/obama.transcript.
6. Psalm 78:4; see verses 1–7.

8. Gain respect (Joshua 4:14)

1. A key exponent of this view is Barbara Kellerman in *Followership: How Followers Are Creating Change and Changing*

Leaders (Harvard Business Review Press, 2008), and *The End of Leadership* (HarperBusiness, 2012).

2. Paul makes this point from the opposite end when he says that he cares little for human judgments and evaluations of his ministry (2 Corinthians 4:3–4). His freedom from such evaluations, however, is balanced by his acute awareness that it is the Lord's judgment that counts.

3. 1 Samuel 24:1–22.

4. 1 Timothy 5:17. The double honour referred to is almost certainly double pay. In my experience this instruction is rarely followed in the contemporary church!

5. Psalm 146:3.

6. Matthew 23:8.

7. 1 Timothy 3:1–7; Titus 1:5–9.

8. 1 Timothy 3:2.

9. See Jonathan Lamb, *Integrity: Leading with God Watching* (IVP, 2006), pp. 16–18.

10. Fred Smith Sr, *Leading with Integrity* (Bethany House, 1999), p. 20.

11. James M. Kouzes and Barry Z. Posner, *The Leadership Challenge*, 4th edn (Jossey-Bass, 2007), p. 37.

12. 'Operation Courage: How to lead when the going gets tough', *Leadership* (Fall, 1999), p. 114.

13. Kouzes and Posner, *Leadership Challenge*, p. 38.

14. Ibid., p. 24. Italics original.

15. Of the seventy-two references to the fool in Proverbs, the following are particularly relevant: 1:7, 22; 3:35; 8:5; 10:10, 18, 21; 12:15, 16, 23; 13:16, 19; 14:3, 8, 16, 17; 15:14; 17:24; 18:2, 7; 20:3.

16. Ecclesiastes 10:5–7. Cf. Proverbs 19:10.

17. 1 Timothy 4:12.

18. 1 Timothy 4:6–16.

19. 1 Timothy 4:15.

9. Surrender status (Joshua 5:13–15)

1. Hugo Young, *One of Us: A Biography of Margaret Thatcher* (MacMillan, 1989), p. vii.
2. Alan Redpath, *Victorious Christian Living: Studies in the Book of Joshua* (Pickering & Inglis, 1955), p. 31.
3. Matthew 5:3.
4. Mark 9:38–41; Luke 9:50.
5. James R. Edwards, *The Gospel according to Mark*, Pillar New Testament Commentary (Eerdmans and Apollos, 2002), p. 290.
6. Matthew 12:30; Luke 11:23.
7. Edwards, p. 291.
8. Ibid., p. 291. R. T. France also points out that the sayings occur in very different contexts, with the person the disciples rebuked apparently being favourable to Jesus, whereas those excluded by Jesus' harsher statement were attributing his exorcisms to Beelzebub. *The Gospel of Mark*, New International Greek Testament Commentary (Eerdmans, 2002), p. 377.
9. Doris Kearns Goodwin, *Team of Rivals: The Political Genius of Abraham Lincoln* (Penguin, 2013), p. 479.
10. Exodus 3:5. This is another point of connection between Moses' and Joshua's leadership.
11. For further details, see David M. Howard Jr, *Joshua*, New American Commentary (Broadman & Holman, 1998), pp. 155–160.
12. Henry and Richard Blackaby, *Called to Be God's Leaders: Lessons in the Life of Joshua* (Nelson, 2004), p. 80.
13. Matthew 5:3, 5.
14. Jeremiah 45:5.
15. SAIACS Chapel Service, 16 March 2016.

10. Trust God (Joshua 6:1–27)

1. Judges 6:1 – 7:25.
2. Genesis 3:1.
3. Dale Ralph Davis, *Joshua*, Focus on the Bible (Christian Focus, 2000), p. 54.
4. John White, *The Fight* (IVP, 1977), p. 97.
5. Ibid., p. 101.
6. David G. Firth, *The Message of Joshua*, The Bible Speaks Today (IVP, 2015), p. 76.
7. Ibid., p. 82.
8. John 2:5.

11. Face failure (Joshua 7:1–9)

1. Warren G. Bennis and Robert J. Thomas, 'Crucibles of Leadership' (Harvard Business Review Press, 2011), p. 99.
2. Ibid.
3. It should be said that this is not always to be viewed negatively, since some ministries, churches and institutions have a season and, having served God faithfully, no longer fit his present purposes. They should be given a decent burial in which we rejoice in what has been accomplished for God. John the Baptist understood this when he said, 'A person can receive only what is given them from heaven' (John 3:27). He had served his purpose, and it was now time for his ministry to disappear and for that of Jesus to become greater. Our human ministries, however blessed by God, are always finite and should never assume his eternal character.
4. Psalm 62:8.
5. Bennis and Thomas, 'Crucibles of Leadership', p. 112.
6. Ibid., p. 99.
7. James 1:2–5.

12. Confront sin (Joshua 7:10–26)

1. See the explanation in ch. 5, p. 35.
2. On the reason for the whole family being punished, see further, Trent C. Butler, *Joshua*, Word Biblical Commentary (Word, 1983), p. 86; David M. Howard Jr, *Joshua*, New American Commentary (Broadman & Holman, 1998), p. 198, and M. H. Woudstra, *The Book of Joshua*, New International Commentary on the Old Testament (Eerdmans, 1981), pp. 130–131.
3. Acts 5:1–11.
4. Acts 8:18–24.
5. 1 Corinthians 5:5.
6. 1 Corinthians 5:9–11.
7. 2 Corinthians 4:10–11.
8. 1 Corinthians 4:18.
9. Matthew 18:6–9.
10. Matthew 18:15–17.
11. John White and Ken Blue, *Healing the Wounded: The Costly Love of Church Discipline* (IVP, 1985), p. 116.
12. Deuteronomy 17:6; 19:15.
13. Galatians 6:1.
14. 1 Corinthians 10:12.
15. 1 Corinthians 13:5–7.
16. White and Blue, *Healing the Wounded*, p. 23.

13. Re-energize people (Joshua 8:1–29)

1. Hebrews 12:10.
2. Joshua 7:4.
3. Judges 7:1–25.
4. Anthony King and Ivor Crewe, *The Blunders of Our Governments* (Oneworld Publications, 2013), p. 249. See pp. 243–253.

5. Ibid., p. 281.
6. Ibid.

14. Renew vision (Joshua 8:30–35)

1. Bill Hybels, *Courageous Leadership* (Zondervan, 2002), p. 31.
2. Ibid., p. 29.
3. Dale Ralph Davis, *Joshua*, Focus on the Bible (Christian Focus, 2000), p. 72.
4. M. H. Woudstra, *The Book of Joshua*, New International Commentary on the Old Testament (Eerdmans, 1981), p. 148.
5. Psalm 72:8, 11.
6. Deuteronomy 27:4.
7. Deuteronomy 27:1–26.
8. The command is given in Exodus 20:25.
9. Woudstra, *Book of Joshua*, p. 148.
10. See also Deuteronomy 17:1–18.
11. I owe this to Trent C. Butler, *Joshua*, Word Biblical Commentary (Word, 1983), p. 95.
12. Exodus 16:33–34.
13. James M. Kouzes and Barry Z. Posner, *The Leadership Challenge*, 4th edn (Jossey-Bass, 2007), p. 143.
14. Ibid., p. 142.
15. Ken Blanchard, *Leading at a Higher Level* (Pearson Education, 2010), p. 19.

15. Correct mistakes (Joshua 9:1–27)

1. M. H. Woudstra, *The Book of Joshua*, New International Commentary on the Old Testament (Eerdmans, 1981), p. 157.
2. E.g. Proverbs 6:6–8; 10:5; 11:14; 15:22; 16:3; 20:4, 18; 21:5.
3. David G. Firth, *The Message of Joshua*, The Bible Speaks Today (IVP, 2015), p. 111.

4. Dale Ralph Davis, *Joshua*, Focus on the Bible (Christian Focus, 2000), p. 79.

5. 2 Corinthians 1:18–20.

6. 2 Corinthians 1:17. See also Matthew 5:34–37; James 5:12.

7. See Judges 11:30–40. Jephthah promised God that if he was granted victory over the Ammonites, on his return home he would sacrifice as a burnt offering whatever first came out of the door of his house to greet him. The first one to do so was his young, virgin daughter. He kept his word and slaughtered her two months after his victory. Should he have done so, or should he have gone back on his word? The story doesn't tell us. We are left to our own judgment. Apart from this being a rash vow that seemed intent on manipulating God, God had prohibited child sacrifice in Israel. Perhaps, then, he should have broken his foolish vow in order to keep the greater commandment of God. This may be an incident where, by keeping his word, he strained out a gnat but, by disobeying God's greater life-giving command, he swallowed a camel (Matthew 23:24).

8. Tony Blair, *A Journey* (Hutchinson, 2010), p. 181.

9. Ibid., p. 184.

10. James M. Kouzes and Barry Z. Posner, *The Leadership Challenge*, 4th edn (Jossey-Bass, 2007), pp. 199–200.

16. Fight battles (Joshua 10:1 – 12:24)

1. This explains why some pastors who are very successful in one church fail in another. Mentally, or emotionally, they've never left the old church and joined the new one. This can become all too painfully evident when they unfavourably compare their present church with their previous one and keep saying, 'In my last church . . .'

2. Joshua 13:1–4.

3. Cf. Joshua 5:13–15.

4. Trent C. Butler, *Joshua*, Word Biblical Commentary (Word, 1983), p. 129.

5. Dale Ralph Davis, *Joshua*, Focus on the Bible (Christian Focus, 2000), p. 95.

6. David M. Howard Jr, *Joshua*, New American Commentary (Broadman & Holman, 1998), p. 271.

7. Howard describes chapter 12 as 'an appendix of sorts to the first major section of the book (chaps. 1–12)'. Ibid., p. 277.

8. 2 Corinthians 4:2.

9. 2 Chronicles 20:15.

17. Demonstrate perseverance (Joshua 13:1–33)

1. Joshua 14:6–15.

2. Joshua 24:29.

3. John 19:30.

4. David G. Firth, *The Message of Joshua*, The Bible Speaks Today (IVP, 2015), pp. 143–144.

5. Land had already been allocated to Reuben, Gad and the half-tribe of Manasseh, east of the River Jordan, so they were not included in this command.

6. Gordon MacDonald, *A Resilient Life* (Thomas Nelson, 2004), back cover.

7. Bill Hybels, *Courageous Leadership* (Zondervan, 2002), p. 231.

8. The levels are set out in ibid., pp. 234–252.

9. Ibid., p. 253.

10. MacDonald, *Resilient Life*, p. 240.

11. Ibid., p. vii.

12. Ibid., pp. 1–14.

18. Manage administration (Joshua 13:8 – 19:51)

1. The New Testament does not explicitly speak of administration as a gift of the Holy Spirit, although some translate *kubernētēs* (lit. 'a pilot') in 1 Corinthians 12:28 in that way. The gift almost certainly refers to a gift of leadership, but is wider than what we understand today as administration. The absence of the word, however, does not imply the gift is unimportant, as is evident from many other parts of Scripture that speak of the careful recording of events and genealogies, the classification of species and the organization of people in the country and serving in the temple (e.g. 1 Kings 4:1–34; 1 Chronicles 22:1 – 27:34).

2. Henry and Richard Blackaby, *Called to Be God's Leaders: Lessons in the Life of Joshua* (Nelson, 2004), pp. 131–132. The authors comment, 'It is striking how meticulous God's instructions were . . . God is that way. He deals in specifics not generalities. His plan for his people was tailor-made down to the last detail.'

3. 1 Peter 1:17.

4. James 3:17.

5. Joshua 13:8, 15, 24, 29, 32, 33; 14:3, 5.

6. Blackaby and Blackaby, *Called to Be God's Leaders*, p. 109.

7. David M. Howard Jr, *Joshua*, New American Commentary (Broadman & Holman, 1998), p. 356.

8. Howard is not completely sure it is an accusation, even though it appears to be. Ibid., p. 360.

9. Butler mentions these two obstacles. Ibid., p. 204.

10. See further, ch. 19.

11. James M. Kouzes and Barry Z. Posner, *The Leadership Challenge*, 4th edn (Jossey-Bass, 2007), pp. 3–26.

12. Ibid., p. 29.

13. Ibid., p. 32.

14. Ibid., p. 33.
15. Ibid., p. 34.
16. Ibid., p. 35.
17. Ibid., p. 37.
18. Ibid., p. 38.
19. Ibid., p. 41.

19. Honour others (Joshua 14:6–14)

1. David M. Howard Jr, *Joshua*, New American Commentary (Broadman & Holman, 1998), p. 330.
2. Judges 1:20.
3. Numbers 13 – 14.
4. See ch. 1, note 16.
5. Henry and Richard Blackaby, *Called to Be God's Leaders: Lessons in the Life of Joshua* (Nelson, 2004), p. 49.
6. Max De Pree, *Leadership Is an Art* (Dell Publishing, 1989), p. 11.
7. James M. Kouzes and Barry Z. Posner, *The Leadership Challenge*, 4th edn (Jossey-Bass, 2007), p. 279.
8. Ibid., p. 292.
9. Ibid., pp. 294–302.
10. De Pree, *Leadership Is an Art*, p. 11.

20. Display compassion (Joshua 20:1 – 21:45)

1. The reason why they were not allocated their own tribal territory can be traced back to Genesis 49:5–7.
2. Daniel Goleman, 'What Makes a Leader?' (Harvard Business Review Press, 2011), p. 3. See also his larger works, *Emotional Intelligence: Why It Can Matter More Than IQ* (Bloomsbury, 2006), and *Social Intelligence* (Arrow Books, 2007).
3. Ibid., p. 3.

4. This paragraph is dependent on ibid., pp. 3, 5 and 16–18.
5. Charles Moore, *Margaret Thatcher: The Authorized Biography*, vol. 1 (Penguin, 2014), pp. 641–642. Italics original.
6. Ibid., p. 642.
7. John 1:47–49.
8. John 2:24.
9. John 6:64.

21. Guard unity (Joshua 22:1–34)

1. Paul is regularly to be seen advocating unity in the church and working for it (Acts 15:1–35; 21:17–26; Romans 14:1–23; 1 Corinthians 1:10–17; Ephesians 4:1–16), but he draws the line when the core gospel of faith is at stake, as in Galatians.
2. Leviticus 17:8–9; Deuteronomy 13:12–15.
3. David M. Howard Jr, *Joshua*, New American Commentary (Broadman & Holman, 1998), p. 406.
4. The law comes in various forms, but was popularized by Robert Merton in 1936 in his essay, 'The Unanticipated Consequences of Purposeful Social Action'.
5. Joshua 18:1.
6. Onora O'Neill, *A Question of Trust* (Cambridge University Press, 2002), p. 18.
7. Numbers 25:6–9.
8. This was akin to Joshua's own action in Joshua 4.
9. O'Neill, *Question of Trust*, p. 18.
10. Ephesians 4:3.

22. Mentor others (Joshua 23:1–16)

1. They are referred to either alone or together in Joshua 3:1 – 4:18; 6:4–16; 7:6; 8:10, 33; 9:15; 17:4; 19:51; 20:1–6; 21:1; 22:13–33; 23:2; 24:1.

2. Joshua 14:1; 17:4; 19:51; 21:1.

3. Thomas Dozeman makes much of this in his commentary on Numbers 27:15–23, and argues that since Joshua's ordination had to be confirmed by Eleazar and he only received part of Moses' authority, Joshua 'will always be subordinate to the high priest'. Perhaps unsurprisingly, the book of Joshua gives no hint about Joshua's subordinate status. But it does portray a non-competitive, collaborative approach. Thomas B. Dozeman and Bruce C. Birch, *New Interpreter's Bible Commentary: Numbers – Samuel*, vol. 2 (Abingdon Press, 1998), pp. 219–220.

4. Joshua 17:4; 21:1.

5. Matthew Syed, *The Times*, 12 September 2016.

6. I am writing this in the year that Leicester, the city in which I live, won the Premier League against all odds, and Wales defied all odds by their success in the European Cup. Both teams have some star players, but when asked the secret of their success, both put it down to the team functioning well together with each member playing his part, not to the star performers.

7. Alex Ferguson with Michael Moritz, *Leading* (Hodder & Stoughton, 2015), p. 87.

8. Ibid., p. 90.

9. Bob Philips, *The Delicate Art of Dancing with Porcupines* (Baker, 1989).

10. Bill Hybels, *Courageous Leadership* (Zondervan, 2002), p. 138.

11. Daniel Goleman cites this as a specific example of where empathy is needed, in 'What Makes a Leader?' (Harvard Business Review Press, 2011), p. 18.

12. James Lawrence, *Growing Leaders: Reflections on Leadership, Life and Jesus* (Bible Reading Fellowship, 2004), p. 226. Lawrence writes an excellent chapter on mentoring, pp. 215–230. Other helpful books about mentoring are Rick Lewis, *Mentoring*

Matters (Monarch, 2012) and Paul Stanley and J. Robert Clinton, *Connecting* (Nav Press, 1992).

13. Lawrence, *Growing Leaders*.
14. 1 Thessalonians 2:8.

23. Keep focus (Joshua 24:1–28)

1. Dale Ralph Davis, *Joshua*, Focus on the Bible (Christian Focus, 2000), p. 177.
2. Joshua 23:1.
3. F. B. Meyer, *Joshua and the Land of Promise* (Morgan & Scott, n.d.), p. 181.
4. Jerome F. D. Creach, *Joshua*, Interpretation (John Knox Press, 2003), p. 129. On this whole section, see pp. 126–130.
5. Meyer, *Joshua*, p. 185.
6. See www.peterkgreer.com.
7. Peter Greer and Chris Horst, *Mission Drift: The Unspoken Crisis Facing Leaders, Charities, and Churches* (Bethany House, 2015), p. 15.
8. Alex Ferguson with Michael Moritz, *Leading* (Hodder & Stoughton, 2015), p. 136.
9. Ibid., p. 167.
10. 2 Timothy 1:6.
11. 2 Timothy 1:14.
12. 2 Timothy 2:1–7.
13. 2 Timothy 2:15.
14. 2 Timothy 2:16–19.
15. 2 Timothy 4:5.
16. Colossians 4:17.
17. 1 Timothy 6:20.

Select bibliography

Books on Joshua

Graeme Auld, *Joshua, Judges and Ruth*, Daily Study Bible (St Andrew Press, 1984)

Henry and Richard Blackaby, *Called to Be God's Leaders: Lessons in the Life of Joshua* (Nelson, 2004)

Trent C. Butler, *Joshua*, Word Biblical Commentary (Word, 1983)

Jerome F. D. Creach, *Joshua*, Interpretation (Westminster John Knox, 2003)

Dale Ralph Davis, *Joshua: No Falling Words*, Focus on the Bible (Christian Focus, 2000)

David G. Firth, *The Message of Joshua*, The Bible Speaks Today (IVP, 2015)

David M. Howard Jr, *Joshua*, New American Commentary (Broadman & Holman, 1998)

F. B. Meyer: *Joshua and the Land of Promise* (Morgan & Scott, n.d.)

Alan Redpath, *Victorious Christian Living: Studies in the Book of Joshua* (Pickering & Inglis, 1955)

M. H. Woudstra, *The Book of Joshua*, New International Commentary on the Old Testament (Eerdmans, 1981)

Books on leadership

Warren G. Bennis and Robert J. Thomas, 'Crucibles of
Leadership' (Harvard Business Review Press, 2011)

Tony Blair, *A Journey* (Hutchinson, 2010)

Ken Blanchard, *Leading at a Higher Level* (Pearson Education, 2010)

Peter Brierley, *Vision Building: Knowing Where You're Going*
(Hodder & Stoughton, 1989)

Max De Pree, *Leadership Is an Art* (Dell Publishing, 1989)

LeRoy Eims, *Be the Leader You Were Meant to Be* (Victor Books,
1975)

Alex Ferguson with Michael Moritz, *Leading* (Hodder &
Stoughton, 2015)

Howard Gardner, *Leading Minds: An Anatomy of Leadership*
(HarperCollins, 1996)

Rudolph W. Giuliani with Ken Kurson, *Leadership* (Little Brown,
2002)

Daniel Goleman, *Emotional Intelligence: Why It Can Matter More
Than IQ* (Bloomsbury, 2006)

————, *Social Intelligence: The New Science of Human Relationships*
(Arrow Books, 2007)

————, *On Leadership*, HBR's 10 Must Reads on Leadership
(Harvard Business Review Press, 2011)

Peter Greer and Chris Horst, *Mission Drift: The Unspoken Crisis
Facing Leaders, Charities, and Churches* (Bethany House, 2015)

Bill Hybels, *Courageous Leadership: Field-Tested Strategy for the
360 Leader* (Zondervan, 2002)

Barbara Kellerman, *Followership: How Followers Are Creating
Change and Changing Leaders* (Harvard Business Review Press,
2008)

————, *The End of Leadership* (HarperBusiness, 2012)

Anthony King and Ivor Crewe, *The Blunders of Our Governments*
(Oneworld Publications, 2013)

James M. Kouzes and Barry Z. Posner, *The Leadership Challenge*, 4th edn (Jossey-Bass, 2007)

Jonathan Lamb, *Integrity: Leading with God Watching* (IVP, 2006)

James Lawrence, *Growing Leaders: Reflections on Leadership, Life and Jesus* (Bible Reading Fellowship, 2004)

Rick Lewis, *Mentoring Matters* (Monarch, 2012)

Gordon MacDonald, *A Resilient Life* (Thomas Nelson, 2004)

Charles Moore, *Margaret Thatcher: The Authorized Biography*, vol. 1 (Penguin, 2014)

Onora O'Neill, *A Question of Trust: The BBC Reith Lectures 2002* (Cambridge University Press, 2002)

Bob Phillips, *The Delicate Art of Dancing with Porcupines* (Baker, 1989)

J. Oswald Sanders, *Spiritual Leadership* (Lakeland, 1967)

Fred Smith Sr, *Leading with Integrity* (Bethany House, 1999)

Paul D. Stanley and J. Robert Clinton, *Connecting: The Mentoring Relationships You Need to Succeed in Life* (NavPress, 1992)

Walter C. Wright, *Relational Leadership: A Biblical Model for Leadership Service* (Paternoster, 2000)

Hugo Young, *One of Us: A Biography of Margaret Thatcher* (Macmillan, 1989)